SAVANNAH

classic

DESSERTS

SAVANNAH *classic* DESSERTS

Recipes from Favorite Restaurants

JANICE SHAY

Foreword by Martha Giddens Nesbit

Photography by Deborah Whitlaw Llewellyn

PELICAN PUBLISHING COMPANY
Gretna 2008

Banana pudding recipe, page 66, reprinted with permission from MRS. WILKES' BOARDINGHOUSE
COOKBOOK by Marcia Thompson and Sema Wilkes. Copyright © 2001 by Marcia Thompson and Sema Wilkes,
Ten Speed Press, Berkeley, CA. www.tenspeed.com.

The word "Pelican" and the depiction of a pelican are trademarks
of Pelican Publishing Company, Inc., and are registered in the
U.S. Patent and Trademark Office.
ISBN-13: 978-1-58980-546-0

Edited by Andrea Chesman, Molly Hall Nagy, Judy Arvites, and Joanna Brodmann

Layout based on a design by Kit Wohl

Printed in Singapore

Published by Pelican Publishing Company, Inc.
1000 Burmaster Street, Gretna, Louisiana 70053

For Patrick, Kerry, and David –
the sweetest and the best.

CONTENTS

Chapter 1 CAKES & TORTES

Chapter 2 COBBLERS, PIES & TARTS

Chapter 3 CUSTARDS, PUDDINGS & SAUCES

Chapter 4 ICE CREAMS & SORBETS

Chapter 5 CHEESECAKES

Chapter 6 CANDIES & COOKIES

FOREWORD

I grew up in the South, and so I thought, at age 21, that I knew everything there was to know about Southern desserts. After all, I had been to quite a few after-the-funeral gatherings, which is where Southern cooks show off their best sweet creations. At the very best funerals, as a show of love and support for the grieving, you could expect to see fried fruit peach pies dusted with powdered sugar, coconut layer cakes, caramel layer cakes, blackberry, blueberry and peach cobblers, pecan and sweet potato pies, banana pudding, killer poundcake and a multitude of cookies, both bar and round.

Then, I moved to Savannah. Fresh out of college with a degree in home economics, I was sure I knew it all when I went to work for the local newspaper as the food writer. Soon afterwards, a handful of Savannah matriarchs took me to a series of lunches at a private club, where I was introduced to desserts that were totally unfamiliar—crème brûlée, crème caramel, and Savannah trifle. Later, at a Savannah restaurant in the historic district, I would be introduced to perhaps my favorite all-time dessert—a benne seed cookie (made with tons of butter, brown sugar and sesame seeds), molded during baking into a "cup," filled with seasonal berries and topped with a thick custard sauce. I am salivating as I write!

What many Savannah classics have in common is that they begin with a custard, the not-so-simple combining of eggs, milk and sugar, slow-cooked until the mixture thickens. The custard can then be topped with brown sugar and broiled for the crème brûlée, or baked on top of melted brown sugar for the crème caramel, or whipped with lots of egg whites and flavored with liqueur before baking to produce the soufflé. And don't forget about probably THE most classic of the Savannah desserts—the trifle—produced by layering custard between sherry soaked cake and whipped cream.

Why the love affair with custard? Because Savannah was settled by the English, and English are known for their custards, and Savannah loves to hang on to her roots. Ask anyone about that.

Another common thread is the Savannah habit of lacing desserts with liqueurs, sherry, bourbon, brandy, and a favorite Savannah wine—Madeira. Madeira arrived in Savannah during the establishment of the colony, brought from the island of Madeira along with grapevines, which were to be grown here. The vines never flourished, but Savannah's love of Madeira certainly did. The wine was not only enjoyed at afternoon wine parties by Savannah's earliest settlers, but it found its way into many dishes, both savory and sweet.

The year 1733, when Savannah was settled by James Edward Oglethorpe, is an awfully long time ago. Savannah today is an international port and a cosmopolitan tourist city whose main attractions are the downtown squares, historic architecture, clever shops offering collectables new, old and artistic, and the beauty of massive live oaks dripping Spanish moss. Then, there is the lure of the water—the Savannah River, which brings international ships past the center of the city, the Intracoastal Waterway, which provides entertainment for small craft from Boston to Florida, and the Atlantic Ocean, which laps at the toes of all those who visit our beloved Tybee Island. When tourists visit, they come hungry, and local chefs are only too happy to take the sweet ideas of the past and give them a new spin.

Although the classic Savannah desserts of old have been modified and modernized in this collection of recipes, there is one thing that is vitally important to their enjoyment—they should always be served in the most elegant dishes you own, and presented with all the flair you can muster. A crème caramel, served in the perfect center of a gold-rimmed china dessert plate, with caramel spilling out all around, is just not the same as crème caramel served on a plastic plate. Savannahians, always appreciative of the natural beauty all around them, are partial to beautiful desserts, artfully presented.

Many writers have written about desserts and their importance to a meal. They are the grand finale, the parting shot, the closing scene, the last hurrah. The dessert is what your guests will remember, and for that reason, I always start with dessert first when planning my menus.

As it turns out, I had a lot to learn about Savannah classic desserts in the beginning, and although I may have not have tasted every single one in the 30 years I have been writing about Savannah food, I have had a delicious time trying! Enjoy!

Martha Nesbit
September, 2007

INTRODUCTION

Life is uncertain, eat dessert first. —Ernestine Ulmer

*Seize the moment. Remember all those women on the Titanic
who waved of the dessert cart.* —Erma Bombeck

Savannah is a city drenched in history. And like many fortunate enough to live in the old South, we remember how to enjoy the "slow life." Taking time for a conversation on the street with an old friend, walking when we don't need to drive (our city was designed for this!), sitting down at the table with family and friends as often as we can, lingering over a meal, and always, of course, enjoying a fabulous dessert—these are some of the ways that Savannahians cherish our Low Country lifestyle.

You will not attend a party, a dinner, a church social, or a festival in Savannah that doesn't count dessert as the centerpiece of the meal. And, it is not unusual to see the dessert buffet visited first, as the erstwhile authors Ulmer and Bombeck behoove us all to do. Savannahians are not a people to pass up a treat or harbor feelings of guilt, so I rarely hear comments about diets when a dessert is offered—and never a refusal! We know that an extra slice of cake just means another brisk walk around Forsyth park tomorrow—both are enjoyable indulgences.

I could not have had a more wonderful time compiling these recipes. Desserts are beloved by most everyone, and I feel sure that there is something to suit every taste in this collection. Whether you're a visitor to the city, or have lived here a lifetime, you will find memories and tastes that remind you of our fair city. Savannah is blessed with many wonderful restaurants, caterers and chefs, who are true artists in their respective kitchens. I thank each and every one for their contributions, and for the enjoyment that these desserts have given and will continue to give.

It was not my intention to write a historic cookbook, although some of these recipes are surely recognizable as ones that matriculated centuries ago from England and other countries. Using the general guideline that a thing may be considered an antique after fifty years (myself included!), I felt that many desserts had been around long enough to be considered classics. Therefore, I make no apologies for including that Northern delicacy, the cheesecake. We've enjoyed it on regional menus for almost a half-century, and these recipes use local ingredients to give it a particularly Southern flavor. Likewise, the Greek baklava recipe that you will find on page 44, while true to its Greek roots, reflects the sizeable, respected Greek population in Savannah that has helped shape the city over the last century.

Pastry chefs are surely the happiest chefs in the kitchen. Each one is secure in the knowledge that their creation puts smiles on peoples faces, and is hardly ever returned to the kitchen uneaten. I'm sure that you will achieve the same happy response when you prepare these dishes for yourself.

Enjoy and don't worry about the calories. Do as our infamous Georgia heroine, Scarlett, did and "worry about that tomorrow"!

Janice Shay
October, 2007

CAKES & TORTES

When Savannahians give a party, they like to lay a fine table. All the family silver, crystal and porcelain will be cleaned, polished and used to decorate a beautiful table. With the many small hidden gardens in the Historic District of the city, hosts often use their flowery spaces to dine outdoors—our own upscale version of backyard dining!

Whatever the setting or the season, the table is never complete without a favorite local dessert. Susan Mason's Red Velvet Cake, or the Cream Cake from Elizabeth on 37th Street are fine examples of classic Savannah sweets. And Martha Giddens Nesbit's Peach Pound Cake is a moist seasonal treat that will disappear far too soon. In fact, better make two of these and hide one for yourself!

Opened in 1981 by Chef Elizabeth Terry, and her husband Michael, this award-winning restaurant is stately Southern elegance personified. True gourmands appreciate the refined atmosphere, along with a menu that emerged from careful research of Southern culinary traditions.

Chef Elizabeth crafted innovative dishes using knowledge of 18th and 19th-century Southern heritage foods. Already a favorite with regional fine diners, national recognition came in the early 90s with awards from magazines like Food and Wine *and the* Wine Spectator. *A peak came in 1995 when she was named the James Beard Perrier Jouet Best American Chef for the Southeast.*

In the last few years, there have been changes, with Elizabeth's brothers now in charge and her culinary protégée Kelly Yambor overseeing the kitchen. Visitors will still see Elizabeth's herbs and edible flowers growing in the house garden out front, and you can be assured of the delicious food that is the trademark of this award-winning Savannah treasure.

ELIZABETH ON 37TH
SAVANNAH CREAM CAKE

SERVES 8 TO 10

NUTMEG ANGEL FOOD CAKE

1/2 cup plus 1 tablespoon cake flour
3/4 cup sugar
1/4 teaspoon freshly grated nutmeg
6 large egg whites
1/2 teaspoon cream of tartar
1/4 teaspoon salt
1/2 teaspoon vanilla extract

SHERRY CUSTARD

1 1/2 teaspoons unflavored gelatin
1/4 cup warm water
2 large egg yolks
1/4 cup good-quality cream sherry
6 tablespoons sugar
1 cup heavy cream
2 teaspoons vanilla extract

FROSTING & BERRIES

1 cup heavy cream
2 tablespoons sugar
1 pint fresh berries (blueberries, raspberries, strawberries)

Preheat the oven to 375° F.

To make the cake, sift together the flour, 1/4 cup of the sugar, and nutmeg and set aside.

Beat the egg whites until frothy, then add cream of tartar and salt. Beat again until soft peaks form. With the mixer running, slowly add the remaining 1/4 cup sugar, 2 tablespoons at a time. Fold in the vanilla and the cake flour mixture. Pour the batter into an ungreased tube pan. Bake for 30 minutes. Invert to cool. When completely cool, remove from the pan. Cut into 1-inch cubes and place in a large bowl.

To make the sherry custard, sprinkle the gelatin over the warm water in a small bowl and set aside.

Beat the egg yolks in an electric mixer with the wire whip attachment until pale. Stir in the sherry and 4 tablespoons of the sugar. Pour into a medium saucepan. Over medium heat, stir the custard constantly until large bubbles appear on the surface and custard is thick. Whisk in the gelatin mixture and continue to whisk vigorously until the gelatin is completely dissolved. Place the pan over a bowl filled with ice and stir until the mixture is cool but not set up.

In a separate bowl, whip the cream with the remaining 2 tablespoons sugar and vanilla. Fold into the cooled custard.

To assemble, fold the custard into the cake pieces. Spoon the cake mixture into an 8-inch springform pan. Refrigerate for at least 2 hours to set.

Just before serving, whip the cream with the sugar. Remove the sides of the springform pan and place the cake on a serving plate. "Frost" with the whipped cream and serve with the berries.

Martha Giddens Nesbit is Savannah's best-known native cook, with books, television appearances and a catering business on her list of accomplishments. For the past few years, she has been busy co-authoring cookbooks with Paula Deen, owner of The Lady and Sons.

Whenever your menu calls for a perfectly elegant, family-friendly dish, Martha is sure to know which seasonal recipe works best, where to get the freshest ingredients, and the Savannah restaurant that serves a decent version of it. She is a veritable encyclopedia of regional recipes, and should be declared a "local treasure." I would tell you her cell phone number, but then she would be too busy to answer my calls for recipes!

MARTHA GIDDENS NESBIT'S
PEACH POUND CAKE

Martha writes, "Using my sour cream pound cake recipe from my first cookbook, *Savannah Collection*, and peaches that were ripe, but not too ripe, I created this recipe. If the peaches are really ripe, you'll have to drain most of the delicious juices or your cake will be too soggy. If your peaches are too hard, don't use them—they simply don't have any flavor. If you can't get perfect peaches, use canned. Regardless of the type of peaches, the pound cake will be very moist and a little gooey on the bottom. The lemon glaze adds a little tangy sweetness and is pretty."

1 cup unsalted butter, at room temperature
3 cups granulated white sugar
6 large eggs
1 cup sour cream
3 cups all-purpose flour, sifted
1/2 teaspoon baking soda
1 teaspoon vanilla extract
1 teaspoon almond extract
2 cups fresh or canned finely chopped and
   well-drained peaches (see Note)

LEMON GLAZE (see Note)
1 1/2 cups confectioners' sugar
1/4 cup fresh lemon juice

Preheat the oven to 300° F. Butter and flour a 10-inch tube pan.

TO MAKE THE CAKE, combine the butter and white sugar in an electric mixture with a paddle attachment. Beat until well combined. Scrape down the sides of the bowl and cream again. Add the eggs, beating well. Scrape down the sides and beat again, until the batter is smooth. Add the sour cream and beat well.

Combine the flour and baking soda and fold into batter. Add the vanilla and almond extracts and beat until just blended and batter is smooth. Stir in the peaches. Pour the batter into the prepared pan. Smooth the top. Lift up the pan and drop it gently onto the counter to get rid of any air pockets.

Bake for 1 1/2 hours. Do not open the oven during this time. The cake is done when the top of the cake is nicely browned, the sides pull away from the pan, and a tester inserted near the center will come out clean. If the cake isn't done after 1 1/2 hours, turn the temperature up to 325° F, bake for 10 minutes more, and test again.

Allow the cake to sit in the pan for about 20 minutes, undisturbed. Loosen the edges of cake from pan with a knife. Invert the cake onto plate, then invert back onto a wire rack to completely cool. Gently transfer to a cake plate.

TO MAKE THE GLAZE, whisk together the confectioners' sugar and lemon juice until smooth. Glaze the cake while still warm, but not hot. Spoon over the top of the slightly warm cake. The glaze will harden when it dries.

NOTE: Two 16-ounce cans of peaches yields 2 cups of chopped peaches. If the humidity is high, the glaze will remain "gummy." You'd be better off not using the glaze and just serving the cake naked, with a dollop of whipped cream.

Soho South Cafe was opened in 1997 in an old auto repair shop. Soho was named for the art neighborhood in New York City, where Retsas lived for 25 years. Lovers of art and the eclectic are drawn to this art gallery turned bistro, but the real find here is the food. Owner and Chef Bonnie Retsas has created a menu of traditional American dishes with a continental flair (and a bit of the South thrown in for good measure).

There's an airy, sunny, flea market atmosphere with every corner filled with one-of-a-kind collectables for sale. Patrons enjoy browsing through the books, gifts and original art while waiting for a table during the always crowded lunch hours. Don't be wary—it's always worth the wait!

SOHO SOUTH CAFE
BERRY SHORTCAKE

SERVES 12

SHORTCAKES

2 large eggs
1 cup heavy cream, plus more if needed
1 tablespoon vanilla extract
4 cups all-purpose flour
1/2 cup granulated white sugar
4 teaspoons (aluminum-free) baking powder
1 teaspoon salt
1 cup unsalted butter, cut into cubes
coarse sugar, to sprinkle

TOPPING

24 ounces fresh berries (raspberries, blackberries, strawberries, or blueberries or a combination of any or all)
2 (16-ounce) bags frozen berries (raspberries, blackberries, strawberries, or blueberries or a combination of any or all)
3/4 cup granulated white sugar
2 cups heavy cream
1/4 cup confectioners' sugar
2 teaspoons vanilla extract

Preheat the oven to 400° F. Line a baking sheet with parchment paper.

To MAKE THE SHORTCAKES, lightly beat the eggs. Mix in the cream and vanilla. Set aside.

Whisk together the flour, white sugar, baking powder, and salt in a large bowl. Toss in the cubed butter. Transfer all of the butter plus about half of the remaining flour mixture into a food processor and pulse until the butter is the size of small peas. Dump the contents of the food processor back into large bowl. Make a well in center and add most of egg mixture, holding back about 1/4 cup of it in case you don't need it all (depending on humidity conditions of the room and the flour). Use a large rubber spatula to combine the mixture without overmixing. If necessary, to make a moist dough, add some or all of the remaining egg mixture. Knead in the bowl three or four times. Transfer the dough to a lightly floured surface. Flatten the dough into a rectangle, fold in thirds letter style, flatten, and repeat this step twice. Then flatten the dough to a thickness of 1 inch. Cut into rounds with a 2 1/2-inch cutter. Brush the tops with a little cream or some of the egg mixture, if any left. Sprinkle with coarse sugar and place on the prepared baking sheet.

Place the shortcakes in the oven and immediately lower the oven temperature to 350° F. Bake for 15 to 20 minutes, until the shortcakes are golden brown.

To MAKE THE BERRY TOPPING, put the fresh berries in a large bowl and sprinkle with sugar. Defrost the frozen berries for 1 minute in a microwave and add to the fresh berries. Mash them with a whisk or potato masher.

To MAKE THE WHIPPED CREAM, beat the cream with the confectioners' sugar and vanilla until soft peaks form. To serve, split the warm shortcakes and put about 1/2 cup berries on the bottom half of each. Spoon some whipped cream on each and place the top halves of the shortcakes on top. Repeat with berries and whipped cream.

SWEET POTATO TORTE

SERVES 12

TORTE

4 medium-size sweet potatoes
ground cinnamon
freshly grated nutmeg
3 1/2 cups cake flour
4 teaspoons baking powder
3/4 teaspoon salt
1 1/4 cups unsalted butter, room temperature
2 cups granulated white sugar
3/4 cup brown sugar
3 large egg yolks
1 cup sour cream
1 tablespoon vanilla extract

2 teaspoons finely grated lemon zest
1 1/2 cups whole milk
8 large egg whites

WHITE CHOCOLATE CREAM CHEESE FROSTING

1 1/2 cups chopped white chocolate chips
1/2 cup cream or milk
2 (8-ounce) packages cream cheese, room temperature
4 cups confectioners' sugar
chopped pecans, to garnish

TO MAKE THE TORTE, boil the sweet potatoes in water to cover until the sweet potatoes are easily pierced with a fork, about 25 minutes. Let cool, then peel and puree or mash. Season to taste with cinnamon and nutmeg.

Preheat the oven to 350° F. Butter and flour three 9-inch cake pans with 1 1/2-inch high sides.

Sift the flour, baking powder, and salt into medium bowl.

Beat the butter in an electric mixer with a wire whisk attachment at high speed until light and fluffy. Gradually add 1 3/4 cups of the white sugar, the brown sugar, egg yolks, and sour cream, beating just until well blended. Beat in the vanilla and lemon zest.

Add the flour mixture alternately with the milk in three additions, beating well after each addition. Beat in the sweet potatoes.

Using clean, dry beaters, beat the egg whites in another large bowl until soft peaks form. Gradually add the remaining 1/4 cup white sugar, beating until stiff but not dry. Fold the whites into the batter in three additions. Divide the batter among the prepared pans.

Bake the layers for about 20 minutes, until golden and a tester inserted near the center of one of the layers comes out clean. Cool the layers in the pans on wire racks for 15 minutes. Cut around the pan sides and turn the layers out onto racks. Turn the layers right-side up and cool completely. (The torte layers can be made 1 day ahead. Wrap in aluminum foil and store at room temperature.)

TO MAKE THE FROSTING, melt the white chocolate with the cream in the top of a double boiler set over simmering water, stirring until smooth. Beat the cream cheese in with an electric mixer (with wire whisk attachment) until smooth and creamy. Beat in the confectioners' sugar and melted chocolate mixture until thick. Let cool.

TO ASSEMBLE THE TORTE, using a serrated knife, cut off the mounded tops of the torte layers to make them level. Place one torte layer on a platter, trimmed side up. Spread with the frosting. Top with a second torte layer, trimmed side up. Spread with the frosting. Top with the third torte layer, trimmed side down. Frost the remaining top and sides. Garnish with chopped pecans.

Sweet Potatoes is the follow-up creation from Steve and Nancy Magulias, owners of Toucan, another unique restaurant on Savannah's Southside. It's billed as "endearing food," with an eclectic and healthy take on traditional Southern favorites.

There's kitchen alchemy at play to turn heavy soul food into lighter, yet still tasty versions of old favorites. A staple flavor is "jerk" seasoning, which hints at the owners' penchant for the sweet and peppery flavors of the Caribbean.

The old-timey decor and casual kitchen table feel make it popular with families. With the Sweet Potato of the Day, chefs get creative with this versatile root vegetable, using it in salads, chili, stuffing or corn bread. Sweet Potatoes serves up the Southern dishes everyone loves.

If you're among the few remaining people in America who've never heard of Paula Deen, then let me introduce you to her wonderful restaurant, The Lady and Sons. It has been a fixture in downtown Savannah since 1997, and is now a destination for travelers from around the world.

Tourists used to stop me on the street and ask where to find the Mercer House, from the book, Midnight in the Garden of Good and Evil; *now, they ask locals, "Where is Paula Deen's restaurant?"*

The Lady and Sons had its humble beginnings back in June 1989 when Paula Deen started The Bag Lady out of her home. The Lady and Sons opened its doors downtown on January 8, 1996. In December 1999, the restaurant was named "International Meal of the Year" by USA Today.

Since November 2003, the restaurant has been in its new location. The new building is a renovated 200 year-old, three-story building with 15,000 square feet of dining, a full service bar and office space. Paula Deen has magnified her restaurant's popularity with her television shows and specials, numerous cookbooks, and a magazine. The popularity of her food is so reknown that the lines start forming at the restaurant door in the early morning, and last late into the night. Don't even try to make reservations—they don't take them. Just enjoy the scene and talk to all the interesting people in line next to you. It's worth the wait!

LADY AND SONS
PUMPKIN GOOEY BUTTER CAKES

Paula Deen is famous for food that reminds you of childhood and home. This is her scrumptious version of a dessert that is finger-lickin' good, to borrow a phrase from another famous Southerner.

SERVES 12

FILLING

1 (8-ounce) package cream cheese, at room temperature
1 (15-ounce) can pumpkin
3 large eggs
1 teaspoon vanilla extract
1/2 cup unsalted butter, melted
1 (16-ounce) box confectioners' sugar
1 teaspoon ground cinnamon
1 teaspoon freshly grated nutmeg

CAKE

1 (18.25-ounce) package yellow cake mix
1 large egg
1/2 cup unsalted butter, melted

whipped cream, to serve

Preheat the oven to 350 ° F. Lightly grease a 9-inch by 13-inch baking pan.

TO MAKE THE CAKE, combine the cake mix, egg, and butter in an electric mixer with a paddle attachment. Beat at medium speed until smooth. Pour into the prepared baking pan.

TO MAKE THE FILLING, beat the cream cheese and pumpkin in a large bowl until smooth. Add the eggs, vanilla, and butter and beat until well mixed. Add the confectioners' sugar, cinnamon, nutmeg, and mix well. Spread the pumpkin mixture over the cake batter.

Bake for 40 to 50 minutes, until the top feels firm. Be careful not to overbake because the center should be a little gooey.

Serve with fresh whipped cream.

VARIATIONS

PINEAPPLE GOOEY CAKE: Omit the pumpkin. Drain 1 (20-ounce) can crushed pineapple and add to the cream cheese filling. Proceed as directed above.

BANANA GOOEY CAKE: Omit the pumpkin. Prepare the cream cheese filling as directed, beating in 2 ripe bananas. Proceed as directed above.

PEANUT BUTTER GOOEY CAKE: Use a chocolate cake mix instead of the yellow cake mix. Add 1 cup creamy peanut butter to the cream cheese filling instead of the pumpkin. Proceed as directed above.

Susan Mason is a caterer extraordinaire, working out of her lovely Victorian home in downtown Historic Savannah and her kitchens in Ardsley Park. Her food is elegant, upscale, and perfectly suited to the genteel Savannah parties in and around the Historic district. And the weddings and large parties that she caters are the stuff of dreams.

I have never been to one of Susan's catered events where she didn't impress everyone with her scrumptious desserts, and this Red Velvet Cake is lovely to look at and a real crowd-pleaser. It is elegant and a real Southern charmer, just like Susan!

SUSAN MASON CATERING
RED VELVET CAKE

This cake is very special for holidays such as Valentine's Day, Christmas or the Fourth of July. Susan claims she can never keep enough red food coloring in the shop at those times!

SERVES 12

CAKE

1 cup buttermilk
1 teaspoon white vinegar
1 teaspoon baking soda
2 1/2 cups self-rising flour
1 teaspoon unsweetened cocoa powder
1/2 teaspoon salt
1 1/2 cups vegetable oil
1 1/2 cups sugar
2 large eggs
2 tablespoons red food coloring
1 teaspoon pure vanilla extract

CREAM CHEESE FROSTING

1 (8-ounce) package cream cheese, softened
1/2 cup (1 stick) unsalted butter, at room temperature
1 (16-ounce) box confectioners' sugar
1 teaspoon vanilla extract
1 cup pecan pieces, chopped
pecan halves, for decoration (optional)

Preheat the oven to 300 F. Grease and flour two 9-inch cake pans. Tap out any excess flour.

To MAKE THE CAKE, combine the buttermilk, vinegar, and baking soda in a medium mixing bowl. Into a second mixing bowl, sift together the flour, cocoa, and salt.

In a large mixing bowl, combine the oil, sugar, and eggs. Beat with an electric mixer on high speed for 3 to 4 minutes, until thickened.

Alternately add the flour mixture and buttermilk mixture to the egg mixture, beating for a least 2 to 3 minutes after each addition. When all the ingredients have been added to the bowl, beat for another 3 to 4 minutes on high speed. Mix in the red food coloring and vanilla until smooth.

Divide the batter equally between the two cake pans.

Bake on center rack in the oven for about 45 minutes, until a tester inserted in the center of the cake comes out clean.

Cook 10 minutes in the pan. Turn out onto a wire rack and let cool completely before frosting.

To MAKE THE FROSTING, combine the cream cheese, butter, confectioners' sugar, and vanilla in a medium-size mixing bowl. Mix with an electric mixer on high speed for 3 to 4 minutes, until completely combined and smooth. Add the pecan pieces and mix until just combined.

Frost the first cake round on top about 1/2 inch thick with frosting, avoiding the edges by about 1/2 inch. Put the second cake round on top and press slightly to line up with the first round. Frost the sides, then the top. Decorate with pecan halves, if desired.

NOTE: The frosting can be made one day ahead of time. Cover with plastic wrap and store in the refrigerator. Bring to room temperature before frosting the cake. You can substitute walnuts for the pecans.

RUM RUNNERS
Hummingbird cake

SERVES 8

3 cups unbleached all-purpose flour
2 cups granulated sugar
1 teaspoon salt
1 teaspoon ground cinnamon
1/2 teaspoon baking powder
3 large eggs, beaten
1 1/2 cups vegetable oil
1 (11-oz) can crushed pineapple, with juice
2 cups diced bananas
2 cups pecans
1 1/2 teaspoons vanilla extract

ICING

1 (8-ounce) package cream cheese, at room
   temperature
1 teaspoon vanilla extract
4 1/2 cups confectioners' sugar
milk (optional)

Preheat the oven to 350° F. Butter two 9-inch cake pans.

To make the cake, combine the flour, sugar, salt, cinnamon, and baking powder in a large bowl. Mix until well blended with a wire whisk. Add the eggs and oil and stir with a wooden spoon until moist. Add the pineapple, bananas, pecans, and vanilla. Stir until well blended. Pour into the prepared pans.

Bake for 25 minutes, until a tester inserted near the center of one of the cakes comes out clean.

Cool on a wire rack for 10 minutes. Invert onto the racks and remove the pans. Finish cooling before frosting.

To make the icing. beat the cream cheese and vanilla until very soft. Add the confectioners' sugar gradually, beating until fully blended and a soft spreading consistency has been reached. Add a little milk if necessary to achieve a spreading consistency. Spread over the top of one layer. Set the second layer on top and frost the top and sides of the cake.

This lovely, old-fashioned bakery is a taste of the Southern past with specialty sweets made from recipes passed down from original owner Ann Rogers' family. The name recalls a time of pirates and sea merchants bringing exotic rums and spices through the old Savannah harbor. The traditional rum cakes are a longtime holiday favorite of customers.

Owner Mary Anne Goljdics moved the bakery from Wilmington Island to Habersham Plaza to increase foot traffic. She credits the popularity of this expanding bakery to quality over quantity— high-grade cocoa, real butter and top-shelf spirits.

New offerings include a Carolina truffle and a specialty low-sugar chocolate torte. Kids love to come pick out a 25-cent treat from the expanding selection of cookies.

The great thing to know about Rum Runners is that they still make everything the old-fashioned way—from scratch.

Canasta cake

SERVES 12

BUTTERCREAM ICING
1/2 cup unsalted butter, at room temperature
1 pound confectioners' sugar
1/3 cup milk
1 teaspoon vanilla extract

CAKE
1 (18.25-ounce box) devil's food cake mix
3 large eggs
1 1/3 cups water
1/3 cup vegetable oil

CHOCOLATE GLAZE
2 (5-ounce) cans evaporated
1 (12-ounce) bag semisweet chocolate

Preheat the oven to 350° F. Butter a 9-inch by 13-inch baking dish.

To MAKE THE CAKE, combine the cake mix, eggs, oil, and water in a large bowl. Beat until well blended. Pour the mixture into the prepared baking dish, making sure the mixture is level. Bake according to directions on box. Cool the cake in the pan for 10 minutes. Then invert onto a wire rack to finish cooling.

To MAKE THE FROSTING, cream the butter with the confectioners' sugar until well blended. Add the milk and vanilla and beat together until smooth.

To MAKE THE GLAZE, pour 1 can of the evaporated milk into a glass bowl. Add half the chips and heat in the microwave until the chips are melted. Stir to blend. Continue stirring in more chips or more evaporated milk, whichever is needed, until the mixture is thick and smooth

To ASSEMBLE THE CAKE, pipe the buttercream icing around the edge of the top of the cake. Pour the chocolate glaze over the entire top of the cake. When the glaze has set, carefully move the cake onto a cake board. Decorate the top with the remaining buttercream as desired.

VARIATIONS
Instead of serving the cake whole, slice the cake into 1-inch by 2-inch finger food servings. Pour chocolate glaze over each and let set. Then decorate as desired with the buttercream.

"All I really need is love, but a little chocolate now and then doesn't hurt!"

—CHARLES SCHULTZ

GALLERY ESPRESSO
GLUTEN-FREE BLUEBERRY BUNDT CAKE

There is always a gluten-free dessert on the menu at this great coffee shop, and this one is a popular favorite.

SERVES 8

CAKE

- 1 1/2 cups confectioners' sugar
- 1 1/3 cup unsalted butter, at room temperature
- 5 large eggs
- 1 3/4 cups white rice flour
- 2 teaspoons baking powder
- 1 cup fresh blueberries

DRIZZLE

- 1 1/2 cups confectioners' sugar
- 1 cup unsalted butter, at room temperature
- 1/3 cup fresh lemon juice

Founded in 1993, this cafe moved a few years ago from a cozy, cavernous location on Liberty to a large, bright spot on Bull Street with a fabulous view of the nearby square. Owner Judy Davis remodeled the building to carry on the ambiance of a classic coffeehouse, adding fireplaces, comfortable old bistro tables and armchairs, and refitting the 100-year old wooden bar.

Daily desserts revolve in a retro-style dessert case, which displays a plethora of choices. Always a popular haunt of students, the mix of patrons now includes locals, tourists, and business professionals, all enjoying the laid-back atmosphere, the food, and of course, the coffee.

Each morning Davis chooses the coffee flavor of the day. The bustle of customers continues into the evening, especially if there's an art opening. The walls of this gallery/coffeehouse continuously display the work of emerging artists, and just like the flow of daily customers, it is always changing.

Preheat the oven to 350° F. Butter a 9-inch bundt pan.

To MAKE THE CAKE, combine the confectioners' sugar and butter in an electric mixer fitted with a wire whisk attachment. Beat at medium-high speed for about 5 minutes, until light and fluffy. With the mixer at medium speed, add the eggs, one at a time, beating until fully incorporated. Add the rice flour and baking powder and mix at medium speed until thoroughly blended. Fold 1 cup fresh blueberries into the batter and pour into a standard bundt pan.

Bake for 30 to 45 minutes, until a tester inserted near the center of the cake comes out clean.

Let cool in the pan for 10 minutes on a wire rack. Invert the cake onto the rack, remove the pan, and finish cooling right-side up.

To MAKE THE DRIZZLE, combine the confectioners' sugar, butter, and lemon juice in an electric mixer with a wire whisk attachment. Beat at high speed until thick. Chill for 30-45 minutes to stiffen. Spoon the drizzle into a piping bag.

To SERVE, slice the cake into eight pieces. Pipe the drizzle in a flower pattern over each piece.

> *"I feel the end approaching. Quick, bring me my dessert, coffee and liqueur."*
>
> —Brillat-Savarin's great aunt Pierette

GALLERY ESPRESSO
COFFEE ALMOND STREUSEL CAKE

SERVES 8

1 3/4 cups all-purpose flour
1 cup granulated white sugar
1 tablespoon baking powder
3/4 cup half-and-half
1/2 cup unsalted butter, melted
2 large eggs
2 ounces full-strength espresso coffee
1/2 cup chopped almonds

TOPPING

1/2 cup self-rising flour
1/3 cup brown sugar
1 teaspoon ground allspice
4 teaspoons very soft butter
confectioners' sugar

Preheat the oven to 350° F. Line a 9-inch cake pan with parchment paper and butter the paper.

To make the cake, mix together the flour, white sugar, and baking powder in a medium bowl. Add the half-and-half, butter, and eggs and beat until well combined. Stir in the espresso and almonds and mix well. Pour into the prepared cake pan.

To make the topping, combine the self-rising flour, brown sugar, and allspice together in a small bowl. Add the butter and mix with a fork until the mixture has the consistency of fine crumbs. Sprinkle over the cake. Cover the pan with aluminum foil, leaving the center slightly domed to allow the cake to rise in the oven.

Bake for 15 minutes. Let cool completely, then remove from the pan. Invert the cake so it sits right-side up on a cake plate. Dust the top with confectioners' sugar. Cut into eight pieces and serve.

COBBLERS, PIES & TARTS

Carriage tours through Savannah's Historic District are a delightful step back in time. Guides are well-versed in the history of buildings and gardens, as well as pointing out the best places to eat around town.

A hundred years ago, the ground level of a Federal-style home in the Historic District was traditionally where the kitchen was located. Windows often had neither screens nor glass. It was dangerous to place your pie in a window too close to the street to cool, because someone could easily make off with it.

Decorative wrought iron designs were sometimes mounted in these windows to keep hungry hands out. It's fun to see these pretty little windows underneath steps, and tourists often wonder why they are there. I never see one without thinking about the many scrumptious pies that have sat in that window over the centuries!

Chocolate Pecan Tart with Gentleman Jack Butterscotch Sauce

SERVES 6 TO 8

THE FILLING

3/4 cup light corn syrup
1/2 cup granulated white sugar
3 tablespoons chilled unsalted butter, cut into small pieces
3 large eggs
1 tablespoon Gentleman Jack whiskey
1 cup pecans, chopped and toasted
1/3 cup sliced almonds

GENTLEMAN JACK BUTTERSCOTCH SAUCE

3/4 cup brown sugar
1/3 cup light corn syrup
2 tablespoons unsalted butter
1/3 cup heavy cream
2 tablespoons Gentleman Jack whisky

NUTMEG CRUST
Makes 1 pie or tart crust

1/4 cup all-purpose flour
2 tablespoons whole wheat pastry flour
1 teaspoon freshly grated nutmeg
3 tablespoons chilled unsalted butter, cut into cubes
2 to 3 tablespoons ice water

Preheat the oven to 350° F.

FIRST, PREPARE THE CRUST in a buttered 9-inch tart pan and set aside in the refrigerator while you prepare the filling.

TO MAKE THE FILLING, combine the corn syrup and the sugar in a medium saucepan over medium heat. Bring to a boil, stirring. Continue cooking for about 2 minutes to dissolve the sugar. Remove from the heat and stir in the butter. Cool for several minutes.

Beat the eggs in a bowl with a whisk to break the yolks, then whisk in the syrup and Gentleman Jack. Pour into the chilled pie shell through a sieve to catch any bits of crystallized sugar. Sprinkle with the pecans, then with the almonds.

Bake the pie for 30 minutes, until the edges are firm and the center is set. Cool before serving with the butterscotch sauce.

TO MAKE THE SAUCE, combine the brown sugar, corn syrup, and butter in a small saucepan over medium heat. Bring to a boil, stirring with a wooden spoon. Stir in the cream. Cool and stir in the Gentleman Jack. Serve at room temperature.

Butter a 9-inch tart or pie pan. Set aside.

In the bowl of a food processor (or with your finger tips), combine the flours, nutmeg, and butter. Process until the mixture resembles a coarse meal. With the motor running, slowly pour in the ice water. Process until the mixture begins to form a mass; just a few seconds. Remove from the processor and shape into a flat disc. Wrap in plastic wrap and refrigerate for 30 minutes.

On a floured surface, roll out the dough into a thin circle. Line the prepared pan with the crust. Trim the edges. Refrigerate until you are ready to fill.

Chef and caterer Joe Randall opened his cooking school in 2000 and has been busy sharing his love of the Southern culinary heritage and history ever since. With a jovial demeanor, he seeks to "put a little South in your mouth," and leave you with the skills and knowledge to make your own kitchen a joyful place.

Randall grew up in the North, but was no stranger to traditional Southern dishes. He sought out African-American chefs, and learned the techniques, ingredients and serving styles of the old South.

He's a bit of an evangelist, preaching the gospel of authentic Southern cuisine. A Taste of Heritage, his cookbook of new African-American cuisine, puts the recipes in their historical context and in a Southern vernacular—duck is the "Tastybird," while chicken is the "Yardbird."

Randall's easygoing style makes his classes a favorite with tourists and locals alike. Students learn to make the "mother sauces" along with variations, and he offers cooking tips with the techniques. His school has something for everyone, including a class on creating the classic Low Country Boil.

CHEF JOE RANDALL
BROWN BUTTER PEACH AND PECAN CINNAMON TART WITH A BOURBON CUSTARD SAUCE

Chef Joe's dishes are like good jazz compositions: simple and complex at the same time. It looks like a simple tart, but the tastes are complex and rich.

SERVES 8

TART CRUST	BOURBON CUSTARD SAUCE
3/4 cup unsalted butter	4 large egg yolks
3 large eggs	3 tablespoons sugar
1 1/4 cups plus 1 tablespoon granulated white sugar	1 teaspoon cornstarch
6 tablespoons unbleached all-purpose flour	pinch of salt
1 tablespoon vanilla extract	1 3/4 cups milk, scalded
1 teaspoon ground cinnamon	1 tablespoon bourbon
1/4 teaspoon freshly grated nutmeg	
	2 cups sliced, peeled fresh peaches
	1/3 cup pecans, toasted
	confectioners' sugar, to serve

FIRST, PREPARE THE CRUST in a 10-inch tart pan with a removable bottom and set aside in the refrigerator while you prepare the filling.

Preheat the oven to 350° F.

Melt the butter over medium heat until a brown sediment forms in the pan, about 3 minutes. Set aside to cool.

Combine the eggs, 1 1/4 cups white sugar, and flour in a food processor. Process until smooth. Pour in the warm butter and process briefly until combined. Add the vanilla and process for 5 seconds. Set aside.

Combine the remaining 1 tablespoon white sugar, cinnamon, and nutmeg in a small bowl to make cinnamon sugar.

Pour the egg mixture into the tart pan. Top with the peaches and pecans and sprinkle with the cinnamon sugar.

Bake the tart for 50 minutes, or until the top is light brown. Cool briefly on a cake rack. Just before serving, remove the sides of the tart pan. Dust with confectioners' sugar and serve warm.

TO MAKE THE BOURBON CUSTARD SAUCE, in a mixing bowl, beat the egg yolks and sugar until thickened and pale. Stir the in cornstarch and salt. Gradually stir in milk. Pour the mixture into a heavy saucepan and cook over low heat, stirring constantly, until the mixture thickens and lightly coats the back of a wooden spoon, 10 to 15 minutes.

Remove from the heat and set the pan in a large bowl of ice water to cool, stirring occasionally. Stir in bourbon and refrigerate, covered, until serving.

NORTH BEACH GRILL
PEACH AND BLACKBERRY COBBLER

SERVES 6 TO 8

FILLING

8 cups (2 quarts) fresh blackberries
8 cups fresh sliced peaches
juice of 1 lemon
1 teaspoon ground cinnamon
1/4 teaspoon freshly grated nutmeg
1 tablespoon peach schnapps
1 1/2 cups sugar
1/4 teaspoon ground allspice

CRUST

1 cup unsalted butter, at room temperature
2 large eggs, at room temperature
2 cups sugar
3 cups all-purpose flour
2 tablespoons vanilla extract
1/2 teaspoon baking powder

TO MAKE THE FILLING, put the blackberries and peaches in two separate mixing bowls. To the peaches, add half the lemon juice, the cinnamon, nutmeg, peach schnapps, and 1 1/4 cups sugar. Mix well and set aside. To the blackberries, add the remaining lemon juice, allspice, and 1/4 cup sugar. Mix together carefully; the blackberries can be fragile. Set aside for 30 minutes. Both the peaches and blackberries will make a syrupy liquid.

Using a slotted spoon, layer the peaches in the bottom of a 9-inch by 13-inch baking dish, leaving most of the syrup behind and fully covering the bottom of the dish evenly with peaches. With the slotted spoon, spoon the blackberries into dish evenly covering the peaches and leaving behind most of the syrupy liquid.

Preheat the oven to 350° F.

TO MAKE THE CRUST, combine the butter and sugar in a large mixing bowl and blend with a hand mixer. Add the eggs, one at a time, and mix in after each addition. Add the flour, 1/2 cup at a time, and mix well after each addition. Add the vanilla and baking powder and blend. The resulting crust should be coarse.

The best way to place the crust on top of the fruit filling is by hand. Take a portion of the crust mixture and knead it together, then press to flatten. Place on top of the fruit filling. Repeat the process until the fruit filling is almost completely covered. (If there are some gaps, it will only make the final presentation more appetizing. Some gaps will fill in during the baking process.)

Bake for 1 hour and 15 minutes, or until a toothpick inserted into the crust in several locations comes out clean.

Serve warm or cooled, with ice cream.

A one-room shack on the north end of Tybee Island—just a 20-minute drive from downtown Savannah—inspired a vision of a Caribbean-style beach bar. Partners George Jackson and George Spriggs opened in 1993, with a desire to serve high quality food from a menu inspired by reggae music. It quickly became the hot spot for both locals and tourists.

Part of its charm is the proximity to the beach and its casual atmosphere, but the food keeps everyone coming back. The tiny kitchen turns out the best plantains, fish tacos and crab cakes outside of the Caribbean, and you can't leave without a taste of George Spriggs' fine cobbler. I often get it to go, so that I can take a little bit of the beach home with me!

In the early years it was closed from November to May, but now the live music and scrumptious fare is offered year round. They've also added on to the original shack, with decks and an outdoor bar where patrons in beach wraps can sip on something cool—a unique dining experience.

CHOCOLATE TART WITH MADEIRA COFFEE CARAMEL SAUCE & PISTACHIO ICE CREAM

MAKES TWO 9-INCH TARTS

ALMOND PÂTE SUCRÉE

1 cup butter, at room temperature
1 cup confectioners' sugar
3 large eggs
3 1/3 cups cake flour
3/4 cup almond flour
1/2 teaspoon baking powder

MADEIRA CARAMEL SAUCE

1/2 cup sugar
1/2 cup sugar or corn syrup
1/2 cup water
1 cup Madeira
2 tablespoons brewed espresso

CHOCOLATE FILLING

2 cups heavy cream
1/2 cup granulated sugar
12 ounces dark chocolate, coarsely chopped
1/2 cup whole milk
2 large eggs

For the PISTACHIO ICE CREAM recipe, see page 80

For the TUILE recipe, see page 80

TO MAKE THE ALMOND PASTRY, beat the butter with the confectioners' sugar until light and fluffy. Add the eggs, one at a time, beating until well combined. Add the cake flour, almond flour, and baking powder and mix just to combine. Allow to chill for at least 1 hour, or overnight.

Divide the dough in half. Roll out each half on a lightly floured surface to a round about 1/4-inch thick. Line two 9-inch tart rings or pie pans with the dough and chill for at least 30 minutes.

Preheat the oven to 350° F. Line the pastry shells with parchment paper and fill with beads or dried beans. Bake for 15 minutes, remove the parchment paper and beads or beans. Continue baking for another 15 minutes, or until the pastry shells are dry; there should be little color. Allow to cool to room temperature.

Preheat the oven to 300° F.

TO MAKE THE FILLING, combine the cream and white sugar in a small saucepan and bring to a simmer over medium heat. Pour over the chocolate and stir until the chocolate has melted. In a separate bowl, whisk together the milk and eggs. Whisk into the chocolate mixture. Pour the filling into the baked tart shells. Bake for 20 minutes, or until the filling is set. Allow the tarts to cool to room temperature before serving.

TO MAKE THE CARAMEL SAUCE, combine the sugar, glucose, and water in a small saucepan over medium heat and cook until it turns a light amber color. Remove from the heat and carefully add the Madeira (this will steam). Return to the heat and whisk to remove any lumps. Allow the mixture to cool and add the espresso. Reserve at room temperature.

TO ASSEMBLE, place the tart on a plate, pour caramel sauce next to it, and place a scoop of pistachio ice cream and a cocoa nib tuile on the tart.

Like many cities proud of their history, change comes slowly to Savannah. So, a new restaurant in town, no matter how good, often suffers until a positive buzz makes its way around town. Not so with this this sleek, elegant venue that burst onto the scene in 2007. It is crowded daily, and you'd be wise to make reservations days, if not weeks, in advance of a visit.

Chef Keith Latture, formerly of the Ritz Carlton Company, creates dishes with an emphasis on Southern European cuisine. Chef Latture seeks out ingredients for his menu from farmers, gamers, fishermen, and dairy producers close at hand.

The restaurant is an island of calm beauty off the South end of the equally beautiful Forsyth Park. The old Savannah Bank was transformed through renovation, with a banquette inside and a palm-shaded courtyard.

OLYMPIA CAFE
BAKLAVA

SERVES 12 TO 15

1 3/4 cups sugar
1 1/4 cups water
1 tablespoon honey
1/2 lemon
1 stick cinnamon
2 whole cloves
8 ounces walnuts, ground

4 ounces almonds, ground
1 teaspoon ground cinnamon

1 pound phyllo pastry sheets (found in the freezer section)

2 cups unsalted butter, clarified (see Note)

TO MAKE THE SYRUP, combine 1 cup of the sugar, the water, honey, lemon, cinnamon stick, and cloves in a saucepan. Bring to a boil. Lower the heat and let simmer for 15 minutes. Remove the lemon, cinnamon stick, and cloves and let the syrup cool.

Meanwhile, combine the remaining 3/4 cup sugar, walnuts, almonds, and ground cinnamon in a large bowl and set aside.

Read the directions on the phyllo box carefully. This pastry requires some special care. Lay the phyllo flat, cover with a damp towel, and keep covered except when removing to assemble the baklava. Count out eight sheets, fold, cover, and refrigerate; these will be used for the top of the dish.

Preheat the oven to 250° F.

Using a large pastry brush, butter a 9-inch by 11-inch baking dish. Lay a phyllo sheet on the bottom of the dish, brush with the butter, and repeat, using eight sheets. Scoop a handful of the nut-spice mixture and sprinkle it over the top phyllo sheet. Lay on more sheets, brushing each with butter, and sprinkle with the nut mixture. Continue until all the nuts and phyllo are used. At this point remove the eight refrigerated pieces and spread over the top, brushing butter in between each one. Using a sharp knife, cut the baklava from top to bottom into diamond shapes. Be sure the knife touches the bottom of the pan as you cut. Heat the remaining butter to sizzling and pour over the top.

Bake for about 1 hour, or until golden and flaky. Remove from the oven and spoon the cooled syrup over the entire pastry.

Cool in the pan, then serve.

NOTE: To clarify butter, cut the butter into small pieces and melt over low heat without stirring. Simmer for 10 minutes, then strain the mixture. You will be left with a clear yellow liquid.

Two natives of Greece opened this lively River Street establishment in 1991, after falling in love with Savannah's historic charm. Nick Pappas and Vasilis Varlagas offer traditional dishes and desserts in their authentic Greek Taverna, using family recipes going back generations.

Olympia Cafe is a local favorite, being voted "Best Greek" many times over, but the location on the river attracts many tourists who stop to try the succulent tidbits that Nick often offers to passersby.

It has a family-friendly atmosphere, and I've never been there without seeing half the tables filled with locals and friends. Don't miss the pizza, the gyros or the calamari. And never leave without the melt-in-your-mouth baklava!

If you're lucky, you'll be able to catch sight of one of the large ships that slowly pass down the Savannah River headed for the port. It's a fun Savannah dining experience!

Paula Deen got a phone call one day from a friend that used to own a restaurant on the marsh near Wilmington Island. He thought it might be for sale, and would they be interested?

Paula said, "Hell, Yeah! Talk to my brother, Bubba." Paula and her brother finally had a home for Uncle Bubba's Oyster House, which opened for business in 2004.

Chief among the unique aspects of this wonderful seafood house is the oyster pit on the dining room floor, where guests can see the oyster shuckers shucking, and smell the oysters being grilled.

You may be under the mistaken impression that key lime pie is only for Floridians, but Uncle Bubba's clean, sweet concoction will convince you that it's pure Savannah.

The last time I was there, Paula Deen was using the dining room for the set of her television show. It was fun to know I was sitting on a set while scarfing down some of the best seafood in town.

UNCLE BUBBA'S
BUBBA'S KEY LIME PIE

SERVES 6

CRUST

5 tablespoons unsalted butter, melted
1 1/2 cups graham cracker crumbs
1/2 cup slivered almonds

FILLING

1 (14-ounce) can sweetened condensed milk
1/2 cup Key lime juice
2 teaspoons grated lime zest
2 large eggs, separated
1/4 teaspoon cream of tartar
1/4 cup sugar

Preheat the oven to 350° F.

To make the crust, combine the butter, graham cracker crumbs, and almonds and mix until moistened. Transfer to a 9-inch pie pan and pat along the sides and bottom to form an even crust. Bake for 5 to 10 minutes, until lightly colored. Set aside to cool.

To make the filling, combine the condensed milk, lime juice, and 1 teaspoon of the zest in a medium bowl. Beat in the egg yolks until smooth. Pour the filling into the crust

To make the meringue, beat the egg whites with the cream of tartar until soft peaks form. Gradually beat in the sugar and remaining 1 teaspoon zest until the mixture is stiff. Spoon the meringue over the filling, spread it to touch the edge of the crust all around. Bake for 12 to 15 minutes, or until meringue is golden brown.
Cool before serving.

JOHNNY HARRIS
COCONUT CREAM PIE

SERVES 6

2 cups sugar

4 large egg yolks

1/4 cup all-purpose flour

2 teaspoons cornstarch

3 cups milk

1/2 cup margarine

1 teaspoon coconut extract

1 teaspoon vanilla extract

1 (6-ounce) bag or can coconut flakes

1 baked 9-inch or 10-inch pie shell, homemade
   or store-bought

whipped cream, to serve

toasted coconut, to serve

Combine the sugar, egg yolks, flour, and cornstarch in a large mixing bowl and whisk until smooth.

Combine the milk and margarine in a medium saucepan over low heat and simmer until blended. Stir in the egg yolk mixture and simmer for 30 to 45 minutes or until completely blended and smooth. Add the coconut and vanilla extracts. Simmer for 5 to 10 minutes more, or until thoroughly blended. Stir in the coconut flakes and remove from the heat.

Spoon the coconut mixture into the pie shell, let cool, then refrigerate.

When you are ready to serve, top the pie with whipped cream and toasted coconut.

This Savannah institution started life as a humble barbeque shack on the corner of Bee Road and Victory Drive in 1924. Johnny Harris and his partner Kermit "Red" Donaldson grew the business, with their house specialties, barbecue and fried chicken, quickly winning loyal customers.

Johnny Harris expanded to its present location in 1936, where it has stood now for over 70 years. Today's diners relish the old-timey feel of the place, with its hand-painted mural on walls encircling the dining room.

The Donaldson family took over the business in the fifties, and Red started marketing the restaurant's signature barbecue sauce. Truly a down home concoction, the recipe originated with a former black cook by the name of John Moore.

Still a family-run business, Red's son Phil heads Donaldson Enterprises, which has expanded the sauce line, along with catering and a chain of restaurants. But for generations of Savannahians, its flagship Johnny Harris restaurant holds cherished of courting, and memorable nights of dining out.

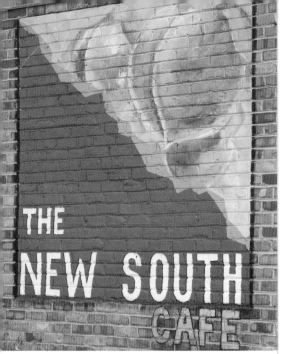

New South Cafe offers Southern food with an edge, with unexpected combinations of ingredients, and an always-artful style of presentation.

Chef Matthew Cohen grew up in an old Jewish-Savannah family going back five generations. He left Savannah and trained at the Culinary Institute of America, where he met his friend and business partner Chef Scott Gordon. New South Cafe evolved out of Cohen's Professional Chef Service, a regional catering company since 2003. The chef-partners opened New South Cafe in 2006, and have since won many awards, including first place at the Taste of Savannah event.

The vibrantly colored, artsy cafe off Skidaway Road, creates an upbeat, casual place just right for such innovative cuisine. These are two young chefs with a mission, and they've established a Catering for Charity plan that has worked well for local fundraising efforts.

Chef Matt Cohen says he cooks because he loves to make people happy. This recipe does the trick!

NEW SOUTH CAFE
PEACH CREAM PIE WITH PEACH BRÛLÉE AND A BLACKBERRY DRIZZLE

SERVES 4 TO 6

CRUST

1 3/4 packages graham crackers
3/4 cup unsalted butter, melted
6 tablespoons granulated white sugar

PEACH PUREE

8 ounces fresh peaches, peeled and diced
1/2 (750-ml) bottle peach wine
4 cups granulated white sugar
pinch of salt
pinch of black pepper

For BLACKBERRY SAUCE, see page 68
For PEACH BRULÉE, see page 68

PASTRY CREAM

4 cups milk
1 1/2 cups granulated white sugar
1 1/8 cups all-purpose flour
1/2 cup cornstarch
8 large egg yolks
4 whole large eggs
1/4 cup unsalted butter

PEACH CREAM FILLING

1/2 cup firmly packed brown sugar
4 cups heavy cream
7 tablespoons granulated white sugar
1 tablespoon vanilla extract

Preheat the oven to 300° F.

TO MAKE THE CRUST, grind the graham crackers in a food processor until you have fine crumbs. Combine the crumbs with the butter and white sugar and mix by hand until well incorporated. Transfer to a 9-inch pie pan and press down along the sides and bottoms to form a pie shell.

Bake for 15 to 20 minutes, until golden brown. Set aside to cool.

TO MAKE THE PEACH PUREE, combine the peaches, peach wine, white sugar, salt, and pepper in a large saucepan. Bring to a boil, reduce the heat, and simmer until the peaches are soft. Puree with a handheld immersion blender and continue to let simmer until the mixture thickens and has the consistency of jam. Keep warm.

TO MAKE THE PASTRY CREAM, combine the milk and 3/4 cup of the white sugar in a saucepan and bring to a boil. Keep warm.

Combine the flour, cornstarch, and remaining 3/4 cup white sugar in a bowl and beat with a whisk to remove any lumps. Add the eggs and beat until smooth. Very gradually add about one-third of the hot milk mixture to the eggs to temper it. Then pour the egg mixture into the remaining hot milk. Bring to a boil, stirring constantly. Remove from the heat, stir in half of the peach puree, and let cool.

TO MAKE THE PEACH CREAM FILLING, combine the remaining warm peach puree with the brown sugar.

Combine the heavy cream, vanilla, and white sugar in an electric mixer with a wire whip attachment. Whip until stiff peaks form. With a rubber spatula, gently fold in the remaining peach puree and the pastry cream until well combined. Pour this mixture into the prepared crust and refrigerate until cold. Garnish with peach brûlée .

POLK'S FRESH MARKET
PECAN TARTLETS

These perfect little pecan pies are simply the best you'll ever put in your mouth—flaky, thin crusts and the simplest of ingredients equal pure pleasure.

SERVES 6 TO 8

1 (9-inch) pie crust, homemade or store-bought
1 1/2 cups chopped pecans
1/2 cup dark corn syrup
1/2 cup firmly packed brown sugar
1/2 cup granulated white sugar
1/4 cup water or bourbon (or mix of both, or substitute brandy for the bourbon)

4 large eggs
1/4 cup unsalted butter, melted
2 teaspoons vanilla extract
1/2 teaspoon salt

Preheat the oven to 325° F. Line a baking sheet with aluminum foil.

Fit the pie crust into a pie pan. Sprinkle the pecans in the pie crust. Set aside.

Combine the light and dark corn syrups, brown and white sugars, and water in a saucepan over medium heat. Bring to a boil and continue to boil for 3 minutes, stirring constantly. Remove from the heat.

Whisk together the eggs, butter, vanilla, and salt in a bowl. Gradually whisk about one-quarter of the corn syrup mixture into the egg mixture. Pour the egg mixture into the remaining hot mixture, whisking constantly. Pour the filling into the pie crust. Set the pie on the prepared baking sheet.

Bake for 55 minutes, or until the filling is just set. The pie will continue to set as it cools. If edges start to get too dark as the pie bakes, fold the foil up around just the edges until done.

Let cool before serving.

VARIATION: Add chocolate chips or coconut along with pecans.

Nature's colorful abundance spills out of this open-air market with hanging baskets out front, and rows of plump red tomatoes and other local produce inside. The whirring of big fans takes you back to a time when the market was the community meeting place in small towns across America.

The Polk family has been bringing fresh produce to Savannah since the late 1940s. Jerry Polk learned the produce business from his father, who picked up what he knew from his father. Charlie Polk sold produce out of his truck at the original City Market downtown. Later, his son Hezekiah "Hez" Polk ran the last open-air produce stand in that area, off Franklin Square.

Polk's Fresh produce now thrives on the spacious corner of Habersham and Liberty. It's still family-run, with his wife Diana, sister Rebecca and other members all working together. Diana whips up lunches, pies, the best cinnamon rolls in town, and lovely fruit and vegetable baskets—all in her tiny kitchen at the back of the market.

Opened in 2002, Avida has already won Best Overall restaurant, with Chef Wes Long named Best Chef in town, by Savannah Magazine. Owner Brian Grenchik oversees the wine list, with more than 100 bottles on and off the menu. Together their refined pairing of wine with meals has garnered attention.

Eclectic music plays in the front of the house—sometimes even French rap—creating a mood right for Savannah's urban sophisticates. Avida has a sleek look, with a stainless steel bar and walls colored in bright reds and blues. There are several large vibrant paintings, including still life portraits by bartender Penelope Moore.

Chef Wes Long creates classical French cuisine with a Southern flair. His specials change with the seasons and the market, and at Avida, all desserts are paired with just the right port or dessert wine.

AVIDA

COUNTRY APPLE AND RIPE PEAR STRUDEL WITH PEPPERCORN CHANTILLY

SERVES 4

STRUDEL

1 sheet puff pastry, thawed if frozen
2 tablespoons unsalted butter, melted
1/4 cup granulated white sugar
1/4 teaspoon cinnamon
2 Granny Smith apples, peeled and diced
2 ripe pears, peeled and diced

CHANTILLY TOPPING

1 cup heavy whipping cream
2 tablespoons confectioners' sugar, or more as needed
1 teaspoon salt
2 tablespoons finely ground tellicherry peppercorns, or more as needed
white pepper (optional)

Fresh blueberries or any seasonal fruit, crushed walnuts, or candied pecans, to garnish

Butter a baking sheet.

To MAKE THE STRUDEL, prick the puff pastry sheet with a fork on both sides. Brush both sides of the pastry with melted butter. Combine the white sugar and cinnamon and sprinkle about half the mixture on both sides of the buttered pastry.

Combine the apples and pears with the remaining cinnamon mixture. Divide the mixture into four equal parts.

To ASSEMBLE THE STRUDEL, place one portion of the fruit mixture on the pastry and fold the pastry over, crimping the edges with your fingers. Repeat three times, until you are out of fruit. Trim off any excess pasty and crimp both ends of strudel with a fork. Place on the prepared baking sheet and refrigerate so the pastry can set back up, at least 30 minutes.

Preheat the oven to 500° F. A convection oven works best.
Bake for 8 to 15 minutes, until golden brown. Let rest before serving.

To MAKE THE TOPPING, whip the cream until soft peaks form. Fold in the confectioners' sugar, salt, and pepper. If you want more spice or sugar, add to taste; white pepper gives it a nice kick without overdoing the pepper.

To SERVE, slice the strudel on the diagonal to create four slices. Place a slice on center of each plate. With a pastry bag, pipe the topping on each plate and garnish with fresh blueberries.

PUDDINGS, CUSTARDS, & SAUCES

In 1733, General James Oglethorpe and the 120 passengers of the good ship "Anne" who had journeyed from England to America, landed on a bluff high along the Savannah River. Oglethorpe named the thirteenth and final American colony "Georgia" after England's King George II, and Savannah became its first city. General Oglethorpe brought with him many English customs and tastes, and arguably, his most important achievement was the city plan with its many beautiful town squares which continue to dazzle visitors today.

The influence of English custards and puddings is still found in many recipes today—most notably, Belford's Creme Caramel and Firefly's Bread Pudding. And there are notable new twists on classic recipes, such as the Sweet Potato Creme Brûlée from Vic's on the River.

Southern Comfort Peach Bread Pudding, with Vanilla Ice Cream & Southern Comfort Creme Anglaise

SERVES 12

BURNT CREAM BATTER

4 cups heavy cream
2/3 cup
8 large egg yolks
1 tablespoon vanilla extract

For CREME ANGLAISE recipe, see page 69

2 1/2 pounds baked cinnamon rolls, cut into 1-inch pieces
4 cups 2 percent milk
1 1/2 tablespoons ground cinnamon
1/2 teaspoon freshly grated nutmeg
1/4 cup Southern Comfort
1/2 cup firmly packed brown sugar
3 pounds frozen and thawed sliced peaches

FIRST, MAKE THE BURNT CREAM BATTER. Scald the cream in a heavy pan over low heat, until the cream reaches 170° to 180° F. Stir occasionally to ensure even heating.

Meanwhile, in a large mixing bowl, beat the sugar and egg yolks together until all of the sugar is dissolved. Stirring constantly, pour the heated cream into the egg mixture. Stir until well mixed. Pour the batter through a Chinoise or fine mesh strainer into a large bowl and skim off any foam. Let cool. Stir in the vanilla.

In a large bowl, soak the pieces of cinnamon rolls in the milk for 10 minutes. Squeeze excess milk from the bread and discard the milk.

In a heavy saucepan, combine the cooled burnt cream batter, cinnamon, nutmeg, Southern Comfort, and brown sugar. Heat the mixture just until all the ingredients dissolve and are well blended.

Preheat the oven to 300° F. Coat a 10-inch by 12-inch baking pan with nonstick spray.

Loosely arrange half the cinnamon rolls in the prepared pan. Do not press down. Lightly chop half the peaches and sprinkle over the first layer of cinnamon rolls. Pour half the liquid mixture over the peaches. Add the remaining cinnamon rolls. Arrange the peaches neatly on top of the bread and then finish with the remaining liquid.

Bake for 30 minutes. Rotate the pan and bake an additional 20 minutes. Cover the pan with foil and continue baking until the juices in the center of the pudding are clear, about 45 minutes.

Serve warm.

Situated on Troupe Square, surrounded by beautiful Federal-style brownstones, this cafe is a favorite with the locals who spill out onto the sidewalk seating, often with their canine friends in tow. In 2002, partners Sharon Stinogel and Lisa Carr opened the sixth restaurant to be established on this corner. It has become one of the most popular spots in the Historic District. The location is charming, the food is great, and the waitstaff is upbeat and happy—they seem to know everyone by name, and are always attentive and helpful.

The vegetarian/vegan fare wins awards, but there are meat dishes and Atlantic seafood to please the omnivore. A top draw is the locally famous Corn Chowder, a warming comfort food when the air is crisp. And the bread pudding, served year-round, is palate-pleasing in any season.

Wholesome food with a gourmet flourish makes this a thriving eatery, with every seat filled during the weekend brunch. Local artists' work hangs on the walls, and ceiling-high windows invite people-watching. It's a place to linger and relax, watch the world go by, and wine and dine in healthy style.

Vic's is housed in a former cotton warehouse designed by New York architect John Norris in 1858. Its multiple stories means there's an entrance on both River and Bay streets, and a perch-like view of the Savannah River and beyond.

Sherman's officers used this building during the War Between the States and left a remarkable piece of history behind. While renovating in 1901, workers found lines drawn on the wall, and soon it was revealed as a map of Sherman's march from Tennessee to Georgia. Visitors to Vic's can see a framed portion of the map, now on display under glass in the main dining room.

Vic's on the River is lively, with music on special evenings and weekends, and a player piano on other evenings. It boasts a solid menu of traditional Southern food, and appeals to many looking for a casual, but classy place with a historic feel. I like the uncluttered feel of the interior, with its yellow walls, and black tablecloths and light fixtures. With the riot of River Street tourists, festivals, musicians, and street artists below, this restaurant is a little piece of heaven on Bay Street.

VIC'S ON THE RIVER
SWEET POTATO CREME BRÛLÉE

SERVES 12

2 sweet potatoes, peeled and cubed
1/2 cup unsalted butter
2 whole vanilla beans
4 cups heavy cream
8 large egg yolks
2 whole large eggs

1 1/8 cups firmly packed brown sugar
1/3 cup granulated white sugar, plus more for dusting
1 teaspoon freshly grated nutmeg
1 teaspoon ground cinnamon

Cover the sweet potatoes with room temperature water in a small saucepan. Bring to a boil and cook until fork tender, about 15 minutes. Drain off the water, add the butter, and mash with a potato masher until whipped with no lumps, set aside.

Preheat the oven to 300° F.

Cut the vanilla beans in half lengthwise and scrape out the beans. Combine the beans and the pods in a saucepan with the heavy cream. Bring this mixture to a simmer.

Combine the egg yolks, whole eggs, brown sugar, white sugar, nutmeg, and cinnamon in a mixing bowl and beat until well combined. Discard the vanilla pods and slowly whisk the hot cream into the egg mixture, adding a little at a time. (This is called tempering. If you add the hot liquid all at once you will have sweet scrambled eggs.) Whisk in the mashed sweet potatoes.

Pour the mixture into eight ovenproof ramekins. Place the ramekins in a shallow baking pan and pour warm water into the pan to a depth of three-quarters up the sides of the ramekins.

Bake for 45 minutes, or until the custard has mostly set.

Place the ramekins in the refrigerator to cool completely.

When you are ready to serve, lightly dust the top of the custard with granulated sugar and blast with a kitchen blowtorch (you can find these in most kitchen supply stores and catalogues) until golden brown. Be careful not to burn the custard, or it will taste bitter.

BELFORD'S
MYERS RUM CREME CARAMEL

Belford's is situated on the City Market, facing a pedestrian street with wonderful shops, cafes, and bars. I always enjoy sitting at a table outside, savoring this sophisticated dish, and watching the town pass by.

SERVES 6

CARAMEL

3/4 cups sugar
1/2 teaspoon lemon juice
1/3 cup water

berries, to garnish
whipped cream, to garnish
mint leaves, to garnish

CUSTARD

1 cup whole milk
1 cup heavy cream
1/2 teaspoon lemon juice
1/4 cup Myers Dark Rum
1/2 cup sugar

TO MAKE THE CARAMEL, combine the sugar, lemon juice, and water in a medium saucepan over medium heat. Cook until the sugar has dissolved. Then bring to a boil, stirring occasionally until mixture caramelizes and turns amber in color; this should take 7 to 9 minutes. Carefully pour the caramel into six ramekins and set aside.

Preheat the oven to 350° F.

TO MAKE THE CUSTARD, combine the milk, cream, and rum in a heavy saucepan over medium heat. Bring to a low boil. Remove from the heat.

Beat the eggs with a whisk in a medium mixing bowl. Gradually whisk in the sugar, and continue to whisk until the mixture is lemon colored. Gradually whisk in one-third of the cream mixture to temper the eggs. Continue adding the cream by thirds, until all is incorporated.

Fill the ramekins with the warm custard. Place the ramekins in a large pan. Fill the pan with hot water until the water reaches halfway up the side of ramekins.

Bake for 30 minutes, or until knife comes out clean.

Transfer the pan to the refrigerator and cool for at least 4 hours, or overnight

TO SERVE, run a knife and around the edge of each ramekin. Place a plate over the ramekin and flip, tap the outer edge of the ramekin, and lift off. Garnish with seasonal berries, whipped cream, and mint leaf.

Belford's is housed in a turn-of-the-century building designed by Hyman W. Witcover. It's considered an architectural standout with its high, arched windows, exposed brick walls and incredible light. It was built for Savannah's Hebrew Congregation in 1902, but sold the following year to W.T. Belford for $23,000.

Belford's Wholesale Food Company was part of the vital and bustling City Market of Savannah for many decades. The framed photographs along the walls are a visual narrative of those days gone by.

Today's City Market is still lively with tourists and the Savannah evening crowd, and Belford's outdoor patio makes for great people-watching. While private parties and receptions bring out its formal side, Belford's offers fine dining in a welcoming, casual atmosphere.

This nationally acclaimed fine dining establishment is founded on the talents of its chef and owner, Christopher Nason. Sapphire's fresh market cuisine is created out of only the finest ingredients, including free-range meats and organic produce. Nason seeks out custom growers of organic heirlooms and wild foods to elevate his cuisine to a fine art.

After being head chef at Bistro Savannah, Nason opened the doors of Sapphire Grill within the brick walls of a 19th-century City Market building. The atmosphere is sleek with stainless steel, accented with an elegant sapphire blue hue.

At Sapphire, Nason offers a creatively eclectic take on Savannah's culinary heritage. As a Chef he's won many honors, including the DiRONA award. He's been featured on the Food Network, Discovery Channel and received accolades from press at every level, including the New York Times, Southern Living and Bon Appetit.

SAPPHIRE GRILL
COCOA-INFUSED CREME CARAMEL

SERVES 6

CARAMEL

1 cup granulated white sugar
3/4 cup water

fresh raspberries, to garnish
confectioners' sugar, to garnish

CUSTARD

8 large egg yolks
1/2 cup granulated white sugar
2 1/2 cups whole milk
1/2 cup heavy cream
1 tablespoon unsweetened cocoa powder
3/4 cup semisweet chocolate chips
1 cinnamon stick
1 vanilla bean

To MAKE THE CARAMEL, combine the white sugar and water in medium saucepan. Bring to a boil. Reduce the heat to medium-high and continue to simmer until the mixture turns to amber or gold. Carefully pour enough caramel into six dry 6 1/2-ounce ramekins to just cover the bottoms. Do not pour in any more than needed. Allow the caramel to cool in the ramekins for 30 minutes.

Preheat the oven to 350° F.

To MAKE THE CUSTARD, whisk the egg yolks and white sugar in a large mixing bowl until pale yellow. Set aside.

Combine the milk, cream, cocoa powder, chocolate chips, and cinnamon stick in a medium saucepan. Split open the vanilla bean and scrape the seeds into the mixture. Drop in the bean. Bring just to a boil over medium heat bring mixture, stirring constantly. Remove the vanilla bean and cinnamon stick.

Temper the egg yolk mixture by gradually adding one quarter of the hot chocolate mixture to the egg mixture while whisking vigorously. Whisk the egg mixture into chocolate mixture. Strain through a very fine mesh sieve.

Divide the custard among the ramekins, filling to just below the top. Place the filled ramekins in a baking pan with sides of 2 inches or higher. Fill the pan with warm water halfway up the sides of the ramekins.

Bake for about 1 hour, or until set. The mixture should barely jiggle when shaken. Allow to cool in the pan in the refrigerator for at least 3 hours.

To SERVE, gently run a paring knife around the inside of each ramekin and invert onto plates. Immediately serve with fresh raspberries and a dusting of confectioners' sugar.

This charming boardinghouse restaurant has been filled with happy diners since it opened in 1943. Mrs. Wilkes, who passed away in 2003, presided over the kitchen and greeted hungry visitors from around the world for more than sixty years. Her excellent traditional Southern food has won national recognition, including the 2000 James Beard America's Regional Classics Restaurant Award.

The Wilkes family continues to operate the restaurant—no longer a boardinghouse— with the same commitment to excellence. Locals and tourists fill the tables daily to get a chance to eat some of the best food in the South.

Everyone shares a bounty of food that is still served boardinghouse-style, and I always enjoy meeting people at the table who are visiting from all over the world. More than once, I've needed to advise doubtful Europeans that, yes, we do eat fried chicken with our fingers.

No matter how much is eaten, no one ever refuses the dessert platter that is passed around. Go for the banana pudding first, because if you are at the end of the table, there may not be any left!

MRS. WILKES
BANANA PUDDING

This is always served at lunches at Mrs. Wilkes', because it is a perennial favorite. Mrs. Wilkes' granddaughter, Marcia, says that for a delicious change, they sometimes substitute pound cake for the vanilla wafers.

SERVES 6

1 (6-ounce) box instant vanilla pudding
1 (7 1/4-ounce box) vanilla wafers
4 bananas. sliced

MERINGUE

2 egg whites
1/8 teaspoon salt
4 tablespoons sugar
1/4 teaspoon vanilla extract

Preheat the oven to 375°.

Make the pudding according to the directions on the box. Arrange the wafers, sliced bananas, and pudding in layers in a 2-quart casserole, ending with a layer of pudding on top. This will make 3 layers.

FOR THE MERINGUE, beat the egg whites and salt until frothy. Add 1 tablespoon of sugar at a time and vanilla, and beat until the meringue is stiff. Spread the meringue gently over the top. Bake for 15 minutes.

NOTE: For a quicker version of this recipe, use pudding as directed on the box and place a layer of whipped cream on top.

BLACKBERRY SAUCE, NEW SOUTH CAFE

4 ounces blackberry puree
1/4 teaspoon honey, or more as needed
6 tablespoons granulated white sugar, or
   more as needed

TO MAKE THE BLACKBERRY PUREE, put the berries in a small saucepan and barely cover the berries with water. Add the sugar and bring to a boil. Decrease the heat and simmer for 5 minutes. Puree in a blender or food processor, then strain out the seeds. Return the puree to a small saucepan and boil to reduce to a good pouring consistency. Let cool, and refrigerate until ready to use.

TO MAKE THE BLACKBERRY SAUCE, combine the blackberry puree and honey in a saucepan. Bring to a boil and boil until it is reduced to a light syrup. Remove from the heat and whisk in the white sugar. Taste and add more honey or sugar if necessary. Set aside and serve at room temperature.

PEACH BRÛLÉE, NEW SOUTH CAFE

1/2 peaches, peeled
1/4 cup granulated white sugar
Salt and black pepper

Partially slice the peach so the slices are still attached at one end. Fan out the peach slices on a baking sheet. Season with salt and pepper. Sprinkle the white sugar evenly over the peach slices. Blast with a blowtorch until the sugar is golden brown. Let the peach rest for a minute to allow the sugar to crystallize. Place on the pie at last minute. Serve the slices drizzled with the blackberry sauce.

Southern Comfort Créme Anglaise, firefly

3 cups heavy cream
4 large egg yolks
1 1/3 cups sugar
2 teaspoons vanilla extract
1/2 cup Southern Comfort
2 quarts premium vanilla ice cream

Heat the heavy cream to boiling in a heavy saucepan.

Whisk together the egg yolks and sugar in a stainless steel bowl. Temper the yolks by adding 1 teaspoon of hot cream to the yolks at a time. Continue doing this until the yolks are warm from the cream. Then mix a little of the yolk mixture back into the cream. Finally, add all of the cream mixture to the yolk mixture.

Place the stainless bowl over a pan of boiling water and cook, stirring constantly with a wire whisk, until the mixture thickens to a light sauce consistency. Remove from the heat and stir in the vanilla.

Cool the sauce in the refrigerator. When cool, stir in the Southern Comfort. Keep refrigerated until needed, but reheat in a double boiler to serve.

Caramel Sauce, belford's

3/4 cups sugar
1/2 teaspoon lemon juice
1/3 cup water

Combine the sugar, lemon juice, and water in a medium saucepan over medium heat. Cook until the sugar has dissolved. Then bring to a boil, stirring occasionally until mixture caramelizes and turns amber in color; this should take 7 to 9 minutes.

ICE CREAMS & SORBETS

Tybee Island lies at the mouth of the Savannah River, a mere twenty minutes by car from the downtown Historic District. It's a palm-filled outpost of casual beach-goers and charming wooden cottages.

In 1736, a 90-foot wooden tower was built to aid navigation in the area. At the time, the tower was the tallest structure of its kind in America. In the intervening years, it has been replaced and improved, and the lighthouse today beckons many to the island, not away from it.

Beach food, picnics, warm weather fare—none of these are complete without ice cream. It is the quintessentially American dessert, and no good coastal city would be without its favorite ice cream shop. Savannah has one of the best in Leopold's Ice Cream, but you can find ice cream treats in every good restaurant from Tybee to Savannah. It is no longer just a summertime indulgence.

Georges' of Tybee was opened in 1998 by George Spriggs and George Jackson, who also own the North Beach Grill on Tybee Island. The partners set out to create a more upscale dining experience, without the pretense – similar to a country inn with a dash of elegance.

The cuisine is Continental with an Asian-French flair, and has gained statewide recognition, as well as rave reviews in Gourmet *and many other national magazines. Chef Robert Wood makes creative use of local seafood, and has been noted for his eclectic preparation style.*

The ambiance is sophisticated, with live music on many evenings. The two Georges hope you'll feel as though you've had a first class meal at a friend's house. High culinary standards and the refined creativity of the food, combined with attentive service keep the loyal clientele coming back.

GEORGES' OF TYBEE
WATERMELON SORBET, ROSEMARY SHORTBREAD & LEMON MASCARPONE

SERVES 4 TO 6

WATERMELON SORBET

1/2 large or 1 small watermelon, juiced (approximately 6 cups)
Juice of 3 lemons
Juice of 2 oranges
3 sheets leaf gelatin or 2 1/4 teaspoons unflavored gelatin
1/2 cup orange blossom honey

LEMON MASCARPONE

1 cup mascarpone cheese
Juice of 1 lemon
1 tablespoon confectioners' sugar

ROSEMARY-BLACK PEPPER SHORTBREAD COOKIES

1/2 cup unsalted butter, melted
1/4 cup pine nuts, toasted
1/2 cup sugar
1 tablespoon chopped fresh rosemary
Freshly ground black pepper
1 cup all-purpose flour

Blueberries or seasonal fruit garnish

To make the sorbet, juice the watermelon using a food mill. Set aside in the refrigerator.

Combine the lemon and orange juices in a nonreactive pan. Add the gelatin and let soften for 5 minutes. Stir in the honey and place over medium heat. Heat until the gelatin is completely dissolved, stirring. Cool in the refrigerator for about 30 minutes.

Add the watermelon juice and return to the refrigerator to chill for another hour, until very cold. Freeze the sorbet by following the directions on your ice-cream maker at home. (If you don't have an ice-cream maker, pour the juice mixture into a shallow baking dish and freeze for 30 minutes. Using a fork, break up the mixture, and return to the freezer for 30 minutes. Continue freezing and breaking up with a fork at half hour intervals, until the mixture is completely frozen.)

To make the cookies, preheat the oven to 350° F. Set out an ungreased baking sheet.

Pour the butter into a mixing bowl. Add the pine nuts, sugar, rosemary, and black pepper to taste. Stir until well mixed. Sift the flour into the mixture and stir to form a stiff dough. Spread out the dough on the baking sheet to a thickness of about 1/4 inch. Pat to make the dough level.

Bake for 17 to 20 minutes, until very lightly browned, rotating the baking sheet halfway through for even baking.

Allow the cookies to cool for a couple of minutes before cutting into a desired shape. Do not let them cool too long or they will crumble when you try to cut them. If this happens, warm them in the oven for a couple of minutes and then try to cut again. Cool completely.

To make the lemon mascarpone, stir together mascarpone, lemon juice, and confectioners' sugar until well blended.

To serve, place a scoop of the sorbet between a couple of cookies on each dessert plate. Either spread the lemon mascarpone on the cookies (as shown), or put on the side for the cookies to be dipped in. Garnish with seasonal fruit or berries.

LEOPOLD'S
HUCKLEBERRY ICE CREAM TOPPING

Leopold's Ice Cream introduced the Huckleberry Sundae as an homage to their neighbor and friend Johnny Mercer, who grew up a block from the original store. Being someone's "huckleberry" was a popular term of endearment in the late 1800s. Johnny Mercer added this expression to his award-winning lyrics for the song "Moon River." Johnny always visited Leopold's when he came home to Savannah. This tradition is carried on today by other Hollywood stars who are friends and colleagues of Stratton Leopold, a veteran Hollywood producer and proprietor of Leopold's Ice Cream.

SERVES 6 TO 8

2 cups fresh or frozen wild huckleberries
1/3 cup sugar
2 tablespoons fresh lemon juice
2 teaspoons cornstarch
1 1/2 teaspoons cold water

Combine the huckleberries, sugar, and lemon juice in a saucepan. Cook, stirring over low heat, until the sugar dissolves and the huckleberries have released their juices. Bring the mixture to a full boil for several minutes, then allow the mixture to simmer for about 5 minutes.

Dissolve the cornstarch in the water and pour into the simmering mixture. Stir slowly for 30 to 60 seconds only. Remove from the heat and allow to cool.

Serve over any combination of ice cream, whipped cream and nuts.

Founded back in 1919, Leopold's was the creation of three immigrant brothers from Greece—George, Peter and Basil. The original location was on the corner of Habersham and Gwinnett, where two streetcar lines intersected. This made it instantly popular, with riders stopping off for a frozen treat.

The three Leopold brothers took what they learned from an uncle about candy and desserts, and eventually perfected the "secret formula" for their ice cream. The famed lyricist Johnny Mercer lived close by, and as a regular customer, promised to write a song about Leopold's Tutti-Frutti ice cream.

In 2004, Leopold's came back to vibrant life when Stratton Leopold—Peter's son—and his wife Mary, re-opened the business. Stratton and Mary are often seen behind the counter scooping ice cream, adding to happy and tasty memories as they continue a beloved Savannah tradition.

Today's Leopold's has many of the original fixtures, giving it the look of an old-fashioned ice cream parlor. The servers wear paper hats, and the ice cream is made on site, using the same secret recipes first concocted all those years ago.

This was the third Alligator Soul restaurant opened by husband-wife Maureen and the late Hilary Craig, after two successful ventures with the same catchy name in the Seattle area. Chef Christopher DiNello passes muster with critics in carrying on celebrated Chef Hilary's tradition of culinary excellence, with everything made on the premises.

The restaurant serves Southern cuisine with a Creole flair, and the menu draws in part on the coastal catch of the season. A wine pairing is carefully selected for each of the daily specials.

Besides being catchy, the owners say that the name Alligator Soul means going beyond judging others by appearances, because the soul is what matters. It's an elegant, yet warm atmosphere, where each patron is made to feel special, and each dish is artfully prepared.

ALLIGATOR SOUL
BANANA BEIGNET

This very simple yet elegant dessert is easy to prepare and sure to please, with its sweet and savory flavors and various textures. Alligator Soul adds candied pecans to their signature dish.

SERVES 4

2 1/2 cups vegetable oil, for frying

BEIGNET BATTER
2 1/4 cups all-purpose flour
1/2 cup cornstarch
1 tablespoon baking powder
1 tablespoon salt
very small pinch of cayenne pepper
3 cups beer

WONTON STICKS
2 tablespoons confectioners' sugar
2 tablespoons ground cinnamon
10 sheets wonton skins

4 large ripe bananas
4 scoops premium ice cream (roasted banana or vanilla)
confectioners' sugar
caramel sauce, heated (recipe, page 69)

Begin heating the oil in deep saucepan to 375° F. Meanwhile, prepare the beignet batter.

TO PREPARE THE BATTER, sift together the flour, cornstarch, baking powder, salt, and cayenne. Whisk in the beer, a little at a time, until the batter has the consistency of heavy cream and will coat the back of a spoon. Allow the batter to rest in the refrigerator for 1 hour.

TO MAKE THE WONTON STICKS, sift together the powdered confectioners sugar and cinnamon. Place the wonton skins on a cutting board, julienne into thin 1/8-inch strips and gently separate. Place in the heated oil and fry until light brown and crisp. Remove from the oil with a slotted spoon and transfer to paper towels to drain. Let cool, then generously sprinkle with the sugar-and-cinnamon mixture, reserving some of the mixture for the final presentation.

TO MAKE THE BEIGNETS, peel the bananas and cut crosswise into 1-inch pieces. Dip each piece into the batter to coat completely. Place the pieces in the heated oil a few at a time, being careful not to crowd. Fry until golden brown. Remove the pieces with a slotted spoon and transfer to paper towels to drain.

TO SERVE, drizzle caramel on the sides and bottoms of four dessert bowls or decorative glasses and place a scoop of ice cream in each. Top the ice cream with five to seven pieces of banana and sprinkle with confectioners' sugar. Top with the crispy wonton sticks and sprinkle the whole dessert with the remaining sugar and cinnamon mixture.

17 HUNDRED 90
STRAWBERRIES ROMANOFF

To enter this wonderful old inn and restaurant is to step back in time. The food is elegant without being fussy, and this charmingly simple dessert is easy to prepare and a year-round crowd-pleaser. The inn is a popular stop on the local ghost tours, so be careful that yours doesn't disappear too quickly.

SERVES 4

3/4 cup fresh strained orange juice (no pulp)
6 tablespoons Grand Marnier
1/2 cup granulated white sugar
1 pint strawberries, hulled and quartered
2 cups heavy cream
1/2 cup confectioners' sugar
1 pint premium vanilla ice cream

Combine the orange juice, Grand Marnier, and sugar in a mixing bowl. Add the strawberries and let marinate for 3 hours.

With a hand mixer, beat the cream with the confectioners' sugar until it forms stiff peaks.

TO SERVE, scoop the ice cream into four dessert bowls. Top with the strawberries and their juice and the whipped cream.

Named the most elegant restaurant in Savannah by Gourmet Magazine*, it's been a fine dining establishment for over 100 years. The building dates to Colonial times, and brick floors and fireplaces add to the rustic, historic atmosphere.*

As the oldest Savannah inn, it's filled with history, along with stories of ghosts wandering its hallways. A lovelorn specter named Anna Powers is said to haunt room 204, and this draws curiosity seekers and ghost hunters as overnight guests.

It's not hard to imagine travelers of bygone eras stopping in for rest and replenishment. Horse-drawn carriages are still bringing folks to the door of the 17 Hundred 90, which carries on a centuries-old tradition of Southern hospitality.

PISTACHIO ICE CREAM, LOCAL 11 TEN

MAKES 2 QUARTS

2 cups half-and-half
4 ounces pistachio paste
2 vanilla beans
6 large egg yolks
1/2 cup sugar
1 cup heavy cream

Combine the half-and-half and pistachio paste in a small saucepan. Slice the vanilla beans in half lengthwise and scrape the seeds into the mixture. Drop the beans in as well. Bring to a simmer over medium heat. Remove the beans.

Whisk together the egg yolks and sugar in a mixing bowl. Slowly add half-and-half mixture to the egg yolks and sugar, whisking while adding. Let cool.

Add the heavy cream. Freeze according to the directions on your ice-cream maker.

COCOA NIB TUILE, LOCAL 11 TEN

MAKES 25

1/2 cup unsalted butter, at room temperature
1/2 cup sugar
4 oz liquid glucose or corn syrup
4 ounces cocoa nibs
3/4 cup all-purpose flour, sifted

Beat together the butter, sugar, and glucose until light and fluffy. Add the cocoa nibs and flour and mix until combined. Divide the mixture into quarters and roll each quarter into a log about 1-inch thick. Wrap in plastic wrap and chill for at least 1 hour.

Preheat the oven to 350° F. Line a baking sheet with a silicone liner or waxed paper.

Work with one portion of dough at a time, remove the dough from plastic wrap and cut into disks 1/4 inch thick. Place each disk on the prepared baking sheet, leaving space for spreading.

Bake for 10 to 15 minutes, just until the centers start to brown. Remove from oven and, using a 1-inch round cookie cutter, cut the center out of each disk. Reserve in an airtight container with waxed paper between layers. Repeat until all the dough is used.

CHEESECAKES

Just because you don't live near a bakery doesn't mean you have to go without cheesecake.

—HEDY LAMARR

CHOCOLATE CINNAMON SWIRL SWEET POTATO CHEESECAKE

SERVES 12

CRUST

11 whole graham crackers, broken
1/4 cup granulated sugar
1/4 cup unsalted butter, melted

CARAMEL-CINNAMON SAUCE

1/2 cup light brown sugar
1/2 cup unsalted butter
1 cup heavy cream

FILLING

6 (8-ounce) packages cream cheese, at room temperature
1 3/4 cups sugar
3 cups cooked mashed sweet potatoes
5 large eggs
3 large egg yolks
1 tablespoon finely grated lemon zest
2 teaspoons vanilla extract
1 teaspoon freshly grated nutmeg
1 teaspoon ground cinnamon
1 1/2 cups semisweet chocolate chips

Preheat the oven to 450° F.

TO MAKE THE CRUST, combine the graham crackers and sugar in food processor and process until fine crumbs form. Add the butter and process until the crumbs are slightly moist. Press onto the bottom (not the sides) of a 9-inch springform pan with 2 1/2-inch sides. Bake until set, about 12 minutes. Transfer to a wire rack; cool completely.

TO MAKE THE SAUCE, melt the butter in a small saucepan over low heat. Add the brown sugar and cook, stirring until dissolved. Add the cream and cook for 2 minutes, then remove from the heat and cool.

TO MAKE THE FILLING, combine the cream cheese and sugar in an electric mixer with a paddle attachment. Beat on low speed until smooth. Add the sweet potatoes, eggs and egg yolks, lemon zest, vanilla, nutmeg, and cinnamon. Beat just until blended. Add the chocolate chips and fold into the batter. Pour the filling into the crust-lined pan. Swirl in half of the caramel sauce.

Bake the cake for 15 minutes. Reduce the oven temperature to 300° F. Bake for about 55 minutes, until the cake is puffed, the outer 2-inch edge is set, and the center moves just slightly when shaken.

Transfer the cake to a wire rack. Run a knife around the pan sides to loosen; cool. Chill the cheesecake overnight. (The cheesecake can be made 2 days ahead. Cover; keep chilled.)

Serve with the remaining caramel sauce.

White Chocolate Pumpkin Cheesecake

SERVES 12

CRUST

2/3 cup graham cracker crumbs
1/4 cup ground almonds
2 tablespoons unsalted butter,
   melted

caramel sauce (optional), page 69

whipped cream, to serve

FILLING

4 (8-ounce) packages cream
cheese, at room temperature
6 large eggs
1 cup sugar
1 (16-ounce) can pumpkin
1 tablespoon ground cinnamon
1 teaspoon freshly grated nutmeg
1/2 teaspoon ground cloves
5 1/3 ounces white chocolate,
   melted
1 tablespoon brandy

Coat a 9-inch springform pan with nonstick pan coating.

To MAKE THE CRUST, combine the graham cracker crumbs and almonds in a medium bowl and stir well. Mix in the melted butter until the mixture just holds together when compressed in your hand. Pat the crust mixture evenly into the bottom of the prepared pan. Set aside while the filling is prepared.

Preheat the oven to 300° F.

To MAKE THE FILLING, beat the cream cheese in an electric mixer with a paddle at low speed until light and fluffy. Add the sugar and beat until just blended. Add the pumpkin, cinnamon, nutmeg, cloves, and the white chocolate and mix until just blended. After each addition, scrape down the sides of the bowl. Drizzle in the brandy. Pour the filling into the prepared crust and smooth the top.
   Bake for 30 minutes. Rotate the pan in the oven and bake an additional 30 minutes. Increase the heat to 325° F and bake an additional 15 minutes, or until a a knife inserted near the center of the cake comes out clean.
   Remove the cake from the oven and cool slowly to room temperature. Refrigerate the cakes for at least 4 hours and up to 12 hours before serving.

To SERVE, slice the cake into twelve pieces, being sure to clean the blade in between each cut. Garnish each slice with a dollop of whipped cream.

B. MATTHEWS
B 52 Cheesecake

SERVES 12

14 ounces heathbar crunch cookies (or your favorite cookies)	1/4 cup fresh lemon juice
	1 tablespoon vanilla extract
	1/4 cup (or 1 airplane bottle) Bailey's Irish Cream liqueur
6 (8-ounce) packages cream cheese, at room temperature	1/4 cup (or 1 airplane bottle) Kahlua or other coffee liqueur
1 cup sugar	1/4 cup (or 1 airplane bottle) Grand Marnier liqueur
7 large eggs	

Preheat the oven to 300° F.

Finely grind the cookies in a food processor. Press firmly into the bottom of a 10-inch springform pan.

Combine the cream cheese and sugar in an electric mixer with a paddle attachment. Beat on medium speed for about 5 minutes, frequently scraping the sides of the bowl with a rubber spatula to ensure that all the ingredients are incorporated. Add the lemon juice and vanilla and mix for 1 minute on medium speed. Mix in the eggs, one at a time, making sure each egg is fully incorporated before adding the next. Divide the batter into three equal parts in three separate bowls.

Mix the Bailey's Irish Cream into the first bowl, the Kahlua into the second bowl, and the Grand Marnier into the third bowl.

Slowly pour the contents of each bowl, one at a time, into the springform pan, layering the ingredients. Place the springform pan in a larger casserole dish and fill with water halfway up the sides of the springform pan.

Bake for 45 to 60 minutes, until firm. Turn off the oven, open the door, and leave cheesecake for another 30 minutes to prevent cracking.

Allow to cool overnight in a refrigerator.

This circa 1792 historic treasure was the first tavern in Georgia, and is the oldest still open for business. Owners Brian and Jennifer Husky have restored it as a popular neighborhood gathering place, open well into the evening.

Its location— just one block from the river—probably explains why this National Landmark building is constructed of old ship parts, some dating back 200 years or more. There's a mast holding up the higher floors, with a slightly curved beam that was once the inner keel of a ship.

Down in its unused cellar, there are working fireplaces and a sand floor, and alongside the walls are iron rings, possibly used to hold slaves just off ships from distant lands. There are rumors of a tunnel in the cellar leading down to the Savannah River, but it is yet to be re-discovered behind the storage from its many past lives.

Today B Matthews is finding new life as a daytime eatery and bistro, with plans for private dining upstairs, and rooftop seating. It has the romantic ambiance of a building haunted by its historic past, while striving to remain a kid-friendly, unpretentious dining experience.

CANDIES & COOKIES

The shingle out front says "Chocolatier" and inside display cases are filled with gourmet varieties imported from 14 countries from Russia to Ecuador, and of course, many from Europe. Owners Gary Hall and Anthony Attardi craved the small town feel after living in Atlanta, and opened their doors to Savannah neighbors and tourists in 2001. Along with the many wonderful chocolates, they offer delightful deli lunch items.

Always willing to draw on local inspiration, a friend's fig preserves are used to caramelize onions for the Baked Chicken Wrap, which is the top selling sandwich in the cafe. The same preserves are used for the Fig Cognac Chocolate Truffles.

A few other assorted chocolate truffles are made on site, along with chocolate-dipped strawberries. Seasonally, they offer chocolate-dipped basil leaves, a rare treat which goes well as an accompaniment to light summer desserts.

Fig Cognac Chocolate Truffles

MAKES 24 PIECES

GANACHE (truffle center)

1/2 cup heavy cream
5 ounces 60 to 70% cacao dark chocolate
3 tablespoons cognac
3 tablespoons fig preserves

COATING

3 tablespoons unsweetened cocoa powder
3 tablespoons sugar

TO MAKE THE GANACHE, heat the cream in heavy–bottomed 1 quart saucepan until small bubbles appear at edges of the pan. Remove from the heat.

Using a food processor, finely chop the chocolate. Transfer the chocolate to a 2-quart bowl. Pour half of the warm cream onto the chocolate, stirring until smooth. Stir in the remaining chocolate, stirring constantly until totally blended. The chocolate should have a slight elasticity to it. If it loses elasticity, add a touch more of the heavy cream, stirring until smooth again. Stir in 2 tablespoons of the cognac. Blend together.

Cover with plastic wrap and cool at room temperature for about 4 hours, or spread onto a clean sheet pan to cool more quickly.

Scrape the chocolate ganache into a 2-quart bowl. Fold in the fig preserves and the remaining 1 tablespoon cognac. Refrigerate for 30 minutes. This will make it easier to roll or scoop truffles into little ball shapes.

TO MAKE THE COATING, mix together the cocoa powder and sugar. To form the truffles, use a small melon baller or tablespoon to scoop up the ganache and form round balls. Roll into the cocoa powder-sugar mixture. Place in the refrigerator again to firm up.

The truffles will last for up to 2 weeks at room temperature in an airtight container.

"The chocoholics 12-step program: Never be more than 12 steps away from chocolate!"

—TERRY MOORE

WRIGHT SQUARE CAFE
PEACH PECAN CHOCOLATE TRUFFLES

MAKES ABOUT 48 TRUFFLES

GANACHE (truffle center)

1/2 cup heavy cream

5 ounces 60 to 70% cacao dark chocolate

2 tablespoons peach schnapps

1/3 cup dried peaches

COATING

3/4 cup finely chopped pecan pieces

2 teaspoons Peach schnapps

TO MAKE THE GANACHE, heat the cream in heavy bottomed 1-quart saucepan until small bubbles appear at edges of the pan. Remove from the heat.

Using a food processor, finely chop chocolate. Transfer the chocolate to a 2-quart bowl. Pour half of the warm cream over the chocolate, stirring until smooth. Stir in the remaining chocolate, stirring constantly until totally blended. The chocolate should have a slight elasticity to it. If it loses elasticity, add a touch more of the heavy cream, stirring until smooth again. Stir in 1 tablespoon of the peach schnapps.

Cover with plastic wrap and cool at room temperature for about 4 hours, or spread onto a clean sheet pan to cool more quickly.

TO PREPARE THE PEACHES, using a food processor, finely chop the dried peaches. Transfer to a bowl and add 2 teaspoons of the peach schnapps. Let sit until the ganache is cooled.

Scrape the cooled ganache into a 2-quart bowl. Fold in the peach mixture and the remaining 1 teaspoon of peach schnapps. Refrigerate for 30 minutes. This will make it easier to roll or scoop the truffles into little ball shapes.

Preheat the oven to 350° F.

TO PREPARE THE COATING, combine the pecan pieces and peach schnapps. Spread out on a baking sheet. Bake for 12 minutes. Let cool.

TO FORM THE TRUFFLES, use a small melon baller or tablespoon to scoop up the ganache and form round balls. Roll in the pecan pieces to evenly coat. Place in the refrigerator again to firm up. The truffles will last for up to 2 weeks at room temperature in an airtight container; up to 2 months if refrigerated.

SOHO SOUTH CAFE
BROWNIE DECADENCE

MAKES 10 TO 12 SERVINGS

1 cup unsalted butter, cut into cubes

8 ounces bittersweet chocolate, coarsely chopped

4 large eggs

1 cup firmly packed dark brown sugar

1 cup granulated white sugar

1/2 teaspoon salt

2 teaspoons vanilla extract

1 cup all-purpose flour

1 cup chopped walnuts or pecans (optional)

Preheat the oven to 350° F. Line a 9-inch by 13-inch pan with aluminum foil. Brush the foil lightly with butter.

Place the cubed butter in a microwave-safe bowl and microwave until completely melted and warm, about 1 minute. Add the chocolate and stir until smooth and glossy. If necessary, return bowl to microwave and heat for an additional 30 seconds.

In another bowl, beat the eggs slightly. Add the brown and white sugars and beat until well blended, about 30 seconds on medium speed if using a hand mixer, about 50 strokes if using a whisk. Do not overbeat. Stir in the chocolate mixture. Add the salt and vanilla. Stir in the flour just until blended. Pour into the prepared pan. Sprinkle the top with the nuts, if using.

Bake for 35 minutes, or until the tip of a small sharp knife inserted near the center comes out almost clean. It should leave just a little chocolate on the knife. The top will be glossy. Do not overbake the brownies or they will be "cakey" and not "fudgy."

Let cool before cutting into squares. Top warm brownie with premium quality ice cream (vanilla, coffee or chocolate), whipped cream, warm chocolate sauce, toasted walnuts and a maraschino cherry.

TWO SMART COOKIES
OATMEAL SCOTCHIES,

MAKES 24 COOKIES

2 cups unsalted butter
2 cups firmly packed brown sugar
1 cup granulated white sugar
3 large eggs
1 teaspoon vanilla extract
2 3/4 cups all-purpose flour

2 1/2 teaspoons baking soda
1/2 teaspoon salt
6 cups old-fashioned rolled oats
1 (10-ounce) bag butterscotch chips
1 cup chopped pecans

Preheat the oven to 350° F. Lightly grease a large cookie sheet.

Combine the butter, brown sugar, and white sugar in an electric mixer with a paddle attachment. Beat until smooth and fluffy. Add the eggs and vanilla and beat until smooth. Add the flour, baking soda, salt, oatmeal, butterscotch chips, and pecans. Mix together well. Scoop with an ice-cream scoop onto the prepared cookie sheet, about 2 inches apart.

Bake for about 8 minutes, until lightly colored. Cool on wire racks.

Annette Rock had proven her baking mettle after many years of gifting her homemade cookies to friends. The business plan for Two Smart Cookies emerged after she met fellow mom Amanda Cannon, while both were cheering on their daughters at volleyball games.

Opened in April 2003, word of mouth has grown their business, which moved to a larger location off White Bluff Road on Savannah's Southside in 2007. Southern Living and Country Living magazines have featured their cookies and whimsical iced cut-outs.

The enticing smell of freshly baked cookies meets customers as soon as they pull up in the parking lot. Designed to look like a farmhouse, the homey and upbeat atmosphere is enlivened by the laughter of children, who are always lining up at the counter eager to try and buy their favorite treats.

RUM RUNNERS
Easy Divinity

MAKES ABOUT 45 PIECES

1 cup egg whites (approximately
   7 large eggs)
1 tablespoon vanilla extract
large pinch of salt

3 1/4 cups sugar
2 cups semisweet chocolate chips
2 cups pecan pieces

Preheat the oven to 350° F. Line three cookie sheets with parchment paper.

   Beat the egg whites with the vanilla and salt in an electric mixer with a wire whisk attachment until foamy. Add the sugar gradually and continue beating until the whites form a stiff peak. Fold in the chocolate chips and pecans.

   Using a small scoop or tablespoon, drop small mounds of the batter onto the prepared cookie sheets. Turn off the oven and put the cookie sheets in. Leave overnight and do not open the oven door for 12 hours. The divinity will become dry and crisp.

RIVER STREET SWEETS
PEANUT BUTTER CUPS

MAKES 6 TO 8 CUPS

1 pound milk chocolate (white chocolate or dark chocolate can be substituted)	peanut butter (creamy or crunchy)

Line 6 to 8 muffin cups with paper liners.

Melt the chocolate in the top of a double boiler, stirring until smooth and glossy. (Alternatively, you can melt in the microwave, heating for 30 seconds at a time, and stirring in between. Do not heat any longer or the chocolate may burn.)

Using an ice-cream scoop and half of the melted chocolate, fill the bottoms of the lined muffin cups with chocolate (not more than 1/3 full). Place a scoop of peanut butter into center of each cup of chocolate. Make sure the peanut butter is no higher than the top of the paper liners. Tap the pan on the counter to help the peanut butter settle into the chocolate. Cover the peanut butter with the remaining melted chocolate. Refrigerate until cool and set.

RIVER STREET SWEETS
SUGAR & SPICE PECANS

MAKES APPROXIMATELY 3 POUNDS

2 pounds pecans	1/2 cup water
3 1/3 cups sugar	1/2 teaspoon ground cinnamon
1/2 cup corn syrup	

Put the pecans in a large metal mixing bowl. The nuts should fill the bowl only halfway.

Combine the sugar, corn syrup, and water in saucepan and stir to combine with a wooden spoon. Place a candy thermometer in the pot and cook the mixture to 240° F. Remove from the heat.

Sprinkle the cinnamon over the hot syrup mixture and mix well. Immediately pour the hot mixture over the pecans and begin folding and stirring, being sure to work all sides of bowl, and pull mixture up from the bottom to assure that all the nuts are sugared. The coating will look clear at first, but it will begin to turn white as it cools and is agitated by folding it into the pecans. Do not stop stirring until the coating has dried. The nuts will still be very hot. Pour the pecans onto a baking tray to cool.

RIVER STREET SWEETS
Peanut Brittle

MAKES APPROXIMATELY 2 POUNDS

1 1/2 teaspoons salt
1 1/2 teaspoons baking soda
2 1/2 cups sugar
1 1/4 cups corn syrup

1 pound unsalted roasted or raw
   peanuts
1 cup water

Coat two large baking trays with nonstick cooking spray. Combine the salt and baking soda in a small cup and blend well. Set aside.

Combine the sugar, corn syrup, and water in a large saucepan (The volume of candy will double or triple when it rises, so use an appropriate pan). Place a candy thermometer in the pan and cook the mixture to 270° F. Stir in the peanuts and continue to cook, stirring continuously, until the mixture reaches 298° F. Keep stirring so that the mixture does will not burn and watch the temperature carefully; it will rise quickly once the peanuts have been added.

Remove from the heat and quickly sprinkle the baking soda and salt mixture evenly over top of hot brittle. Stir until dissolved and well blended. The mixture will start to rise quickly in the pan. Immediately pour the brittle onto the prepared baking sheets. The mixture will continue to expand after pouring so do not overfill the baking sheets. Spread evenly with a spatula.

When the brittle has cooled for 1 minute, using heat resistant gloves, flip it over. Be cautious; the brittle will be very hot at this point.

After about 2 more minutes, cut the brittle in half on each tray. Wearing heat-resistant cooking gloves, stretch the brittle while still pliable.

Allow the brittle to cool completely, then break into random-sized pieces.

NOTE: You can score the brittle with a pizza cutter after stretching, but while still pliable. This will allow you to break it into more uniform pieces.

Walk down the famous River Street and you will be inevitably be drawn to the exquisite smell of candy being made on the spot. It's hard to resist coming in to watch the churning and mixing, and trying a sample (or three)!

In 1973, Georgia Nash and Pamela Strickland first sold furniture and gifts at their store called "The Cotton Bale" in an old River Street cotton warehouse. The mother-daughter partners added an enormous fudge pot a few years later, and this produced the top-seller, as well as fascinating passers-by.

After testing recipes for homemade candy, they perfected the "World Famous Praline," which is now the signature item (and one recipe they won't reveal!). River Street Sweets was born and the demand for their sweet Southern confections is now worldwide. River Street Sweets is a Southern candy store empire.

INDEX

My gratitude and admiration goes to Martha Giddens Nesbit, for the many ways she helped with this book, for her friendship, and her boundless knowledge of Savannah food.

I could not have completed this book without the happy assistance of my friend and colleague, Angela Rojas. Thanks also for the research and editorial help of Andrea Chesman, Molly Hall Nagy, Joanna Brodmann, and Judie Arvites.

Special thanks to Dr. Calhoun and Nina Kooij at Pelican Publishing Company for their encouragement, help and support.

Kudos to Kit Wohl, who authored the first book in this series, *New Orleans Classic Desserts*, and who set the bar high for me. Your book is an inspiration, Kit, and I hope this title does it justice.

And finally, thanks to my friend, Deborah Whitlaw Llewellyn, for her wonderful photography and for eating twelve desserts a day with me while we were shooting. I always give you the difficult jobs, Deborah, and you never complain. God bless you!